Understanding Foucault

Understanding Foucault

Geoff Danaher, Tony Schirato
and Jen Webb

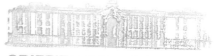

Los Angeles | London | New Delhi
Singapore | Washington DC

© Geoff Danaher, Tony Schirato and Jen Webb 2000

First published 2000 by Allen & Unwin, Australia

First published in Great Britain 2002 by SAGE Publications Ltd

Reprinted 2003, 2005, 2006, 2007, 2009

SAGE Publications Ltd
1 Oliver's Yard
55 City Road
London EC1Y 1SP

SAGE Publications Inc.
2455 Teller Road
Thousand Oaks, California 91320

SAGE Publications India Pvt Ltd
B 1/I 1, Mohan Cooperative Industrial Area
Mathura Road
New Delhi 110 044

SAGE Publications Asia-Pacific Pte Ltd
33 Pekin Street #02-01
Far East Square
Singapore 048763

British Library Cataloguing in Publication Data

A catalogue record for this book is available from the British Library

ISBN 978-0-7619-6815-3 (hbk)
ISBN 978-0-7619-6816-0 (pbk)

Typeset in 10.5/12pt Palatino by DOCUPRO, Sydney, Australia
Printed and bound in Great Britain by The MPG Books Group

Contents

Glossary

archaeology is the term used by Foucault to refer to the process of working through the historical archives of various societies to bring to light the discursive formations and events that have produced the fields of knowledge and discursive formations of different historical periods.

author function is what identifies, categorises and marks a particular discourse or set of discourses, and authorises them to circulate within a society. 'Author' in this sense doesn't refer to the concrete person, but to the 'name' by which we know a particular set of works.

biopolitics and **biopower** refer to the technologies, knowledges, discourses, politics and practices used to bring about the production and management of a state's human resources. Biopower analyses, regulates, controls, explains and defines the human subject, its body and behaviour.

cultural capital can be anything which has value, and is exchangeable, within a cultural field or fields. The production and acceptance of, and changes to, cultural capital are determined within and by specific fields.

descending individualism refers to the way in which, in modern western societies, people are more closely monitored and 'individualised' the lower in the social scale they are.

Under the old order of feudal societies and monarchical rule, the more powerful one was the more watched and noticed one became. 'Descending individualism' operates according to the opposite impulse; prisoners are monitored and individualised by guards, pupils by teachers, children by parents, patients by doctors and so on.

dialectical materialism is a concept derived from the philosophy of Karl Marx. Marx applied Hegel's concept of the dialectic, involving the struggle of opposing forces which might be resolved by the emergence of a new synthesis, to the material economic conditions of society. For Marx, the struggle between the bourgeois property-owning class and the proletariat working class in nineteenth-century Europe would eventually give rise to the emergence of a Communist utopian society.

disciplinary institutions refers to institutions emerging in nineteenth-century Europe such as the prison, workhouse, schools and barracks which took hold of the bodies and minds of their inhabitants and shaped them according to disciplinary procedures and 'quiet coercions'.

discipline refers first to the notion of punishment or coercion, and second to the notion of sets of skills and knowledges which must be mastered in order to achieve success in particular fields. Foucault connects these two meanings through his concept of 'power-knowledge'.

discourse generally refers to a type of language associated with an institution, and includes the ideas and statements which express an institution's values. In Foucault's writings, it is used to describe individual acts of language, or 'language in action'—the ideas and statements that allow us to make sense of and 'see' things.

dividing practices refers to the ways in which social groups are separated from one another on the basis of judgements made about their actions and attitudes. For example, the mad are divided from the sane, the sick from the healthy, the criminal from the legal.

the Enlightenment, for Foucault, is both a collection of ideas and attitudes (concerning reason, justice, equality, progress and rationality) and a series of political events (beginning with the French Revolution). Historically, the Enlightenment sought to replace the old order of absolute sovereignty, injustice, ignorance and superstition with an order based on reason, rationality and equality. More specifically, Foucault understood the Enlightenment as being based on an interrogation of how and what and why things are, and as a particular self-referential attitude to oneself and one's time.

epistemes are periods of history organised around, and explicable in terms of, specific world-views and discourses. They are characterised by institutions, disciplines, knowledges, rules and activities consistent with those world-views. The rise and fall of epistemes doesn't correspond to any notion of natural continuity, development or progress, but is random and contingent.

ethics, in Foucault's definition, refers to how people behave in relation to the 'moral' norms—the sets of rules, prohibitions and codes of a society.

games of truth refers to the sets of rules within particular institutions by which the truth is produced.

genealogy is a process of analysing and uncovering the historical relationship between truth, knowledge and power. Foucault suggests, following Nietzsche, that knowledge and truth are produced by struggles both between and within institutions, fields and disciplines and then presented as if they are eternal and universal.

governing and **government**, for Foucault, can be understood in terms of both a 'body politics'—the ways in which we conduct ourselves, the relationships that we have with our body and other bodies in society—and, in a more conventional sense, the way in which a state rules over its people.

governmentality is the term Foucault uses to describe the change in technologies of, and attitudes towards, governing which developed in Europe in the eighteenth century. This involved a greater emphasis on the state's ability to manage its resources (including its population) economically and efficiently, and a concomitant increase in state intervention in the lives of its citizens. There have been two major consequences of this change. The first is that citizens are both 'regulated' by the state and its institutions and discourses, and educated to monitor and regulate their own behaviour. The second, which derives from what Foucault calls the 'liberal attitude', is the emergence of an understanding, on the part of citizens, of the need to 'negotiate' those forces of 'subject regulation' through a process of 'self-governing'.

habitus is a term used by the French sociologist Pierre Bourdieu, which refers to the ways in which we are produced as subjects through sets of dispositions—or habits—which predispose us to think and behave in ways that are adapted to the structures in which we are constituted. Since these are *pre*dispositions, they are embodied, durable and largely unconscious.

hegemony is the term, developed by the Marxist theorist Antonio Gramsci, which refers to the way in which states and state institutions work to 'win' popular consent for their authority through a variety of processes which disguise their position of dominance.

heterotopia refers to the way in which radically different social spaces can come into connection with one another. For example, the space of the gentlemen's clubs which British colonists established in India was radically different from the social space through which the Indian people moved and made sense of the world.

ideology refers to a system of ideas held by a particular group within a culture and which represents their interests, and the practices whereby such groups attempt to naturalise their ideas, meanings and values, or pass them off as universal and as commonsense.

juridical sovereignty refers to the notion that laws that are reasonable, just, rational and self-evident are (or should be) the driving force and organising principle behind human society.

knowledge, for Foucault, is made up of perspectives, ideas, narratives, commentaries, rules, categories, laws, terms, explanations and definitions produced and valorised by disciplines, fields and institutions through the application of scientific principles. Different and new knowledge emerges from the struggle between the different areas within a culture.

liberalism is an attitude and practice that monitors and works to limit the control, intrusion or intervention of the state in the social, economic and cultural activities of its citizens.

micro-power explains how discourses 'write' the body, or shape the ways in which bodies are understood and function.

modernity as used in disciplines like philosophy, historiography and sociology generally refers to that period of (western) history which dates from the Enlightenment, and which is characterised by scientific rationality, the development of commerce and capitalism, the rise of education, surveillance, urbanism and atheism.

normative judgements are used to assess and monitor the actions and attitudes of people according to the notion of a norm or average. Such judgements work throughout various institutions such as prisons, schools and hospitals, as well as throughout the social body as a whole, to divide the 'normal' from the 'abnormal'.

Oedipus complex is a term taken from psychoanalysis and refers to the child's repressed desire for the mother, and rivalry with the father.

the 'order of things' refers to a combination of the institutions, knowledges, discourses and practices which organise an episteme, and which make some things and activities possible and explicable, and other things unthinkable. The reason for, or the logic of, such 'order' provides the foundation for social practices and systems of social organisation, without necessarily being visible itself.

panopticism refers to Bentham's model of the panopticon, which was a tower placed in a central position within the prison. From this tower, the guards would be able to observe every cell and the prisoners inside them, but it was designed in such a way that the prisoners would never know whether they were being observed or not. Prisoners would assume that they could be observed at any moment and would adjust their behaviour accordingly.

power for Foucault is not a thing that is held and used by individuals or groups. Rather, it is both a complex flow and a set of relations between different groups and areas of society which changes with circumstances and time. The other point Foucault makes about power is that it is not solely negative (working to repress or control people): it is also highly productive. Power produces resistance to itself; it produces what we are and what we can do; and it produces how we see ourselves and the world.

power-knowledge is Foucault's concept that knowledge is something that makes us its subjects, because we make sense of ourselves by referring back to various bodies of knowledge.

social contract theory refers to the notion that people freely choose to submit to the dictates and laws of the state in exchange for its protection.

subjectivity is the term derived from psychoanalytic theory to describe and explain identity, or the self. It replaces the commonsense notion that our identity is the product of our conscious, self-governing self and, instead, presents individual identity as the product of discourses, ideologies and institutional practices.

subjugated knowledge is a form of knowledge that has been subjugated or 'buried' under the official or dominant forms of knowledge that emerge within a social order.

technologies, for Foucault, refers to two main functions or mechanisms: first, the ways in which societies pacify, dominate and regulate subjects; and second, 'technologies of the self', which allow individuals to shape their own bodies and thoughts.

warfare society refers to the idea that all social activity can be explained in terms of struggles between different sections of society. Marxism is an example of this position.

will to power, which Foucault takes from Nietzsche, refers to the notion that meanings, ideas, rules, discourses, knowledge, and 'truths' do not emerge naturally, but are produced in order to support, advantage or valorise a particular social group.

1

Introduction to Michel Foucault's work and contexts

The French cultural theorist Michel de Certeau tells a story about Michel Foucault being bombarded, at a press conference in Belo Horizonte in Brazil, with questions and criticisms concerning his politics, his beliefs, where he was coming from, and what his works 'really meant' (Certeau 1986: 193). This 'interrogation' provoked, according to Certeau, the following response in Foucault's introduction to *The Archaeology of Knowledge*:

> What, do you imagine that I would take so much trouble
> and so much pleasure in writing, do you think that I
> would keep so persistently to my task, if I were not
> preparing . . . a labyrinth . . . in which I could lose myself
> . . . Do not ask who I am and do not ask me to remain
> the same: leave it to our bureaucrats and our police to see
> that our papers are in order. At least spare us their
> morality when we write. (1972: 17)

A great many critics, such as the journalist and historian Robert Hughes, author of *The Fatal Shore*, didn't spare Foucault 'their morality' (there is a detailed description and analysis of Hughes' comments in Chapter 3). Twenty years ago Michel Foucault was probably the most vilified and criticised of all the so-called 'postmodern theorists', today he is widely accepted as being one of, if not the, most influential thinkers of our time, and his ideas and theoretical terms have become part of our ways of thinking and understanding the world.

A great deal of the hostility that was directed at Foucault and his work was part of a more general backlash against a group of predominantly French theorists—figures such as Baudrillard, Derrida, and Deleuze—whose ideas were seen as posing threats and challenges to established fields and disciplines such as history, political economy, philosophy, sociology, literature, geography and psychology. Most of the writers, academics and other professionals in these fields presumed two important things about the knowledge they produced. First, they presumed that it constituted an authentic truth which explained and evaluated many of the important 'hows and whys' of life—everything from the 'reality' of the history of nations to the 'truth' about the human unconscious. Second, they believed that this 'production of knowledge' was part of an ongoing process of civilisation, and was free of political considerations—they were contributing to making the world a better place, in much the same manner as the hard sciences.

Postmodernist theories challenged both these assumptions— knowledge was now seen as being full of contradictions, unanswered questions and cultural prejudices. Instead of official knowledge being the only explanation of things, it was really a case of some explanations winning out over others— often for political reasons (for instance, official, western medicine over traditional remedies from places such as China). Whichever explanations 'won' became knowledge— and therefore 'truth'. And our knowledge wasn't necessarily better than that of other ages—just different. Disciplines and fields were 'advancing' the human race—they were more or less fighting over who could claim to know the truth.

However, while Derrida's work was largely directed against the disciplines of literature and philosophy, Deleuze's against psychoanalysis, and Baudrillard's against political economy, Foucault's work challenged virtually all the main fields and disciplines—which made him a target for historians (who said he didn't get his facts right), novelists and literary academics (who accused him of underestimating the importance of individual genius and inspiration), and Marxists (who didn't like his 'disregard' for economics).

This hostility wasn't confined to the more traditional disciplines. Baudrillard, the most provocative of the postmodern theorists, authored a book entitled *Forget Foucault*. Some writers who were associated with the newer fields of feminist studies and postcolonial studies strongly criticised Foucault for not dealing specifically with what they considered to be the most important issues in western history (the exploitation of women and the enslavement of colonial peoples). And yet, despite these criticisms, both fields are highly indebted to Foucault. The first volume of *The History of Sexuality*, which challenged the notion of a progressive movement in western culture towards 'sexual freedom', made many feminists rethink the relationship between sex, sexuality and identity. And Edward Said's *Orientalism*, probably the most influential book to come out of postcolonial studies, used theoretical approaches and language taken directly from Foucault in order to describe and analyse the ways in which the West 'produced' the concepts of the Orient and the oriental for political purposes.

In the last two decades Foucault's books and theories have been taken up and used not only by academics and students (for instance in cultural studies, history, literature, gender studies, postcoloniality, sociology and philosophy), but also by professionals in areas such as medicine, public health, social work and welfare; law, economics, business management and government; criminology and prison management; media, education, architecture, art and journalism; and computing, public relations and ecology.

Because of this widespread popularity and use of Foucault's work, certain notions of what constitutes the 'principles' of Foucaultian thought and theory have sprung up, principles that have been developed and circulated both by those using Foucault's work, and those criticising it. Sometimes these are highly inaccurate. For instance, one of the ideas associated with Foucault is that people are completely dominated by and subject to power. This usually gets translated into a notion that we are merely the dupes of dominant social groups, never knowing what we do, and therefore unable to resist power—whether it is employed by governments, the ruling classes, capitalism or the ordinary institutions that regulate and control our day-to-day lives. Now there is actually nothing in Foucault's work which conforms to this notion, but that hasn't stopped it from being circulated as one of the 'truths' of Foucaultian theory.

What we are attempting to do in this book is to provide an accurate and accessible introduction to Foucault's work, theories and ideas, most particularly as they apply to our everyday ideas, activities and subjectivities (identities). The chapters that follow are divided into sections which look at various aspects of what we can call the three major Foucaultian 'themes'—knowledge, power and subjectivity. Before getting to them, however, it is worthwhile spending some time looking at where Foucault's work 'came from'—at the major intellectual and theoretical contexts that influenced and helped produce his work and ideas.

Marxism and phenomenology

In the years immediately following the Second World War, when Foucault was attending university and starting out as a scholar, there were two main bodies of theory and knowledge that dominated much of French intellectual life—Marxism and phenomenology. Marxism exerted a considerable influence, both politically and theoretically. During the Cold War years many French university students, including Foucault for a time, became members of the French Communist Party. And the introduction and popularisation of the works of the German philosopher Georg Hegel in France, by theorists such as Alexandre Kojeve and Jean Hyppolite, served to renew interest in Marxism. The two areas—political commitment and activity, on the one hand, and philosophy, on the other—came together precisely because Marxism put itself forward as a philosophy that didn't just think or talk about the world. It wanted to change it, and finish off the 'march to freedom' that, for many French intellectuals, had begun with the French Revolution. What appealed to these French intellectuals was that Marxism, at least in the version that was influenced by Hegel, guaranteed that this would happen—it was inevitable that history would be 'driven and resolved' by the working class. All the violence and irrationality that had characterised the twentieth century (culminating in Nazism, the greatest of all irrationalities) was now to be integrated into and overcome by Marxism, which the prominent existentialist Jean-Paul Sartre described as 'the untranscendable horizon of our times' (Eribon 1991: 20).

The second major influence on French intellectual life at this time was phenomenology, particularly those theories of phenomenology that appeared in the work of Edmund Husserl and Martin Heidegger in Germany, and Maurice Merleau-Ponty in France. According to phenomenology, all meaning was to be found in a person's perception of the 'universal essence' of an object or thing. This led to the 'existential philosophy' of Sartre, who posited the individual as more or less a free agent who was both responsible for and capable of organising experience and making sense of it. From this perspective, all truth came out of the ability of human subjects to consider and understand what was going on around them, including their own involvement in the world— their desires, motivations and activities. Whereas for Marxism irrationality and violence were to be overcome by the 'spirit of history', for phenomenology these 'evils' could be over- come by people coming to full knowledge of the truth (and errors) of themselves and the world.

The history of truth and reason

Foucault became familiar with Marxism and phenomenology because they were the most influential bodies of theory during the postwar years and because of the tremendous prestige of intellectuals (Merleau-Ponty, Sartre, Hyppolite, Heidegger, Kojeve and others) working in these areas. But, by and large, his work can be read more as a reaction against them and their theories. Foucault was far more interested in, and receptive to, work which, instead of trying to understand the 'one and only' truth of things, tried to 'historicise' the different kinds of truth, knowledge, rationality and reason that had developed in cultures.

This tendency on Foucault's part to attempt to contextualise and historicise notions of truth, knowledge, rationality and reason did not sit well with either Marxism or phenomenology, which provided more 'absolutist' and essentialist versions of human activities, ideas and meanings. Most French Marxists understood history as 'teleological'—that is, as unfolding more or less steadily towards a set outcome. All events and ideas could be neatly categorised and evaluated, for many Marxists, in terms of this one story of the inevitable march of history towards the rule of the working classes. Under this concept there were two categories of ideas, science and ideology—the true (Marxism) and the false (bourgeois ideology)—and all social and cultural activity could be explained in terms of the notion of class warfare. Phenomenology was equally 'absolutist'. As phenomenologists understood it, truth and meaning were absolute and essential—they had always been there, and weren't subject to change; they just needed a 'knowing human subject' to bring them to light.

Foucault was more influenced by the 'historicising' work of Martin Heidegger and, most particularly, the 'scientific histories' of Georges Canguilhem. Although Heidegger was a phenomenologist, he emphasised the centrality of the social and cultural contexts in which truth and meaning were produced. For Heidegger, people's ideas and activities were largely determined by the background in which they lived, but this relationship could never really be made clear—people tended to think that they were acting freely and independently of their contexts. Canguilhem's work was concerned with scientific ideas (particularly in the area of biology), but what interested him was the way in which 'scientific rationality and reason' was always changing, and the way that 'bodies of knowledge and truth', which were thought to be 'eternal', could come to an end and be replaced by a different 'truth' or rationality. What Foucault took from these two theorists was first, the notion that what people could know was always limited by their contexts, and second—and relatedly—that what constituted truth and rationality was not inevitable (scientific 'breakthroughs', for instance, often happened by chance) and changed across history.

Structuralism and psychoanalysis

There were two other bodies of theory which influenced French intellectual life, including the work of Foucault, from the 1960s onward—structuralism and psychoanalytical theory. Foucault was aware of the line of structuralist work stretching back to the early twentieth century and including Saussure and Jakobson (linguistics), Boas and Dumezil (anthropology), and the Russian formalists (linguistics and literature). Two other contemporary French theorists, Roland Barthes (litera- ture and semiotics) and Louis Althusser (Marxism and political theory)—who was also one of Foucault's teachers— also exerted an influence on him. *The Order of Things* and *The Archaeology of Knowledge* in particular were read by many critics as structuralist works, though Foucault denied this.

Structuralism offered Foucault two major advances over Marxism and phenomenology. First, according to Foucault it was able to provide the kind of precise and systematic kind of historical analysis (of a work, a body of works or a period of history) that the more 'absolutist' theories could not match. Structuralism's big breakthrough, which it took from the work of Saussure, was to understand meaning as relational. In other words, events, ideas and activities didn't 'mean anything' in themselves—they only made sense when related to other events, ideas and activities. For instance, Saussure made the point that in order to understand what the word 'man' meant in a language, you had to 'relate it' to other words—such as woman, child, boy, girl or animal. The same thing applied to ideas, political events, books, and everyday activities.

The second point that Foucault took from structuralism was what has been called 'the death of the subject'—or, in Roland Barthes' terms, the 'death of the author'. Structuralism extends Heidegger's insight that people are not really free to think and act, because they—and their ideas and activities—are produced by the structures (social, political, cultural) in which they live. According to this perspective, people don't 'think or speak ideas' or make meanings. On the contrary, structures 'think and speak through people'. In fact, the very idea of a 'free subject' is, ironically, a meaning that is produced by a culture, and that controls our thinking and behaviour.

Psychoanalytical theory, especially as developed through the works of Sigmund Freud and, later, Jacques Lacan, continued this critique of the 'free subject'. According to Freud and Lacan, the subject is a kind of myth which comes about when we repress our desires in order to be accepted into society. Like structuralism, with which he was closely identified, and contrary to phenomenology, Lacan theorised that the subject could never know itself—its existence was based on a kind of necessary ignorance.

Although Foucault was influenced by these two bodies of theory, and made considerable use of structuralist techniques of analysis (particularly, as we have already noted, in *The Order of Things* and *The Archaeology of Knowledge*) he differed from them on a number of counts. First, Foucault rejected the notion that structuralist analysis could 'deliver up' the whole meaning of something—a book or a period of history—by analysing all its relevant 'relations'. For Foucault, this method might account for everything that had been included in, say, a period of history, but it couldn't account for (or didn't want to take into account as psychoanalysis did) what was 'not there'—in other words, what was 'repressed', or impossible to think. The second problem with structuralism was its inability to account for change and discontinuity. Like

Saussure's language system, everything was a perfect system, and then it changed to another perfect system—but there was no explanation of how or why this change occurred. Third, again like Saussure's theory of language, structuralism could explain what the 'rules of a system' were (of language, chess, or football), but it couldn't account for people's activities (why people used the rules in one way and not another, for example).

Foucault's problems with psychoanalysis centred on the point that while, on the one hand, it helped to do away with the notion of the 'knowing subject' by introducing the ideas of repression and the unconscious, on the other hand it claimed at the same time to understand and make sense of the 'truth' of the subject. For instance, an important idea in psychoanalysis was that all desire was supposed to be tied to the law of castration and lack, as outlined in Freud's notion of the Oedipus complex. Foucault dealt with this problem in some detail in *The History of Sexuality*, together with his objection to the more general notion that sexuality could be seen as providing the 'truth' about people.

Nietzsche

Perhaps the most important influence on Foucault's work, particularly from *The Order of Things* onward, was the German philosopher Friedrich Nietzsche. We will discuss Nietzsche's contributions in more detail in later chapters, but we can say here that Nietzsche's ideas about the relationship between truth, knowledge and power opened the way for Canguilhem's work on 'the history of science'. Nietzsche rejected the notion that history unfolds in a rational way, with the gradual development of higher forms of reason. Attempts to identify a historical point—say ancient Greece, or imperial Rome—as the origin of an essential idea, way of life or value (democracy, western civilisation, reason) were, for Nietzsche, all about power rather than historical knowledge. In fact, any form of knowledge or truth that emerged in a culture did so,

Nietzsche argued, not because it was valuable or eternal, but because one group had managed to impose their will over others. Whereas Marxism could survey the field of history and come up with a single version of things, Nietzsche would insist that there were many possible stories and developments, but that these alternatives had to be repressed and forgotten so that dominant groups could justify the 'inevitability' of their own rise to power. An obvious example of this occurred at the end of the nineteenth century, when American capitalists explained that they were destined to, and deserving of, power and wealth because they were, in Darwinian terms, 'the fittest', while the poor were biologically unfit to compete with them.

What is Enlightenment?

The final theoretical and intellectual influence on Foucault we will consider is the legacy of the Enlightenment, particularly as it was articulated by the German philosopher Immanuel Kant. In an essay entitled 'What is Enlightenment?', Foucault made it very clear that he did not subscribe to the idea, fashionable in some postmodern theories, of a complete rejection of the Enlightenment. While he had reservations about the politics that had been practiced in the name of the Enlightenment (which we will deal with in Chapter 5), Foucault was of the opinion that it provided something that was extremely useful—the notion of critique. Critique, for Foucault, meant something akin to an investigation into what we are (how we think, what we value, how we understand ourselves, how we treat others), but it also meant thinking what else we might be—how we could be different from ourselves. In other words, what Foucault took from Kant and the Enlightenment was not:

> . . . a theory, a doctrine, nor even a permanent body of knowledge that is accumulating; it must be conceived as an attitude, an ethos . . . in which the critique of what we are is at one and the same time the historical analysis of

the limits imposed on us and an experiment with the possibility of going beyond them. (Foucault 1997: 319)

Foucault's attachment and commitment to this Enlightenment attitude goes a long way towards explaining two significant aspects of his work: first, his rejection of essentialising theories such as Marxism and phenomenology (theories which relied on the idea of an absolute and ahistorical quality, or 'truth'); and, second, his taking up of a specifically 'historicising' perspective when it came to analysing claims to, and notions of, truth and knowledge. And it is also a factor in making sense of his movement from texts (such as *Madness and Civilisation*, *The Order of Things*, *Discipline and Punish* or *The History of Sexuality*) which were primarily concerned with 'denaturalising' discourses and bodies of thought, and describing the 'limitations' placed on what could be known, to a position of 'working through' how individuals might come to terms with, and maybe move beyond, their own historical contexts (*The Use of Pleasure*, *The Care of the Self*).

Conclusion

What we have done in this chapter is to provide a brief introduction to some of the more significant intellectual contexts that influenced, both in a negative and positive sense, Foucault's theoretical development. These include:

- Marxism, a philosophy committed to changing the world and ensuring freedom for the oppressed, and driven by the belief that this future is inevitable, and will be brought into existence through the efforts of the working class;
- Phenomenology, which holds that all meaning is to be found in a person's perception of the 'universal essence' of an object or thing, and hence that truth comes from the ability of human beings to understand the world and their own involvement in the world;
- Structuralism, which understands meaning as relational rather than essential (that is, that things—people, events,

ideas, practices—make sense only when related to other events, ideas or activities) and which developed precise and systematic analytical methodologies;

• Psychoanalytical theory, which critiqued the idea that human beings are free or possessed of inherent and individual qualities and which introduced the idea that identity is produced through repressed desires and the work of the unconscious;

• The work of Friedrich Nietzsche, and his understandings of the relationship between truth, knowledge and power;

• The Enlightenment, with its valuing of reason, justice, equality and progress.

In the following chapters we will describe how these influences were played out in Foucault's work in three main areas: the question of knowledge, relations of power, and the question of the subject.

Further reading

Eribon, Didier 1991, *Michel Foucault*, Faber, London

McNay, Lois 1994, *Foucault: A Critical Introduction*, Continuum, New York, see 'Introduction'

2

Questions of knowledge

The order of things

At the beginning of Foucault's preface to *The Order of Things*, he offers the following explanation as to where the book 'came from':

> This book first arose out of a passage in Borges, out of the laughter that shattered, as I read the passage, all the familiar landmarks of my thought—*our* thought, the thought that bears the stamp of our age and our geography—breaking up all the ordered surfaces and all the planes with which we are accustomed to tame the wild profusion of existing things . . . This passage quotes a 'certain Chinese encyclopaedia' in which it is written that 'animals are divided into: (a) belonging to the Emperor, (b) embalmed, (c) tame, (d) sucking pigs, (e) sirens, (f) fabulous, (g) stray dogs, (h) included in the present classification, (i) frenzied, (j) innumerable, (k) drawn with a very fine camelhair brush, (l) *et cetera*, (m) having just broken the water pitcher, (n) that from a long way off look like flies'. In the wonderment of this taxonomy, the thing that . . . is demonstrated as the exotic charm of another system of thought, is the limitation of our own, the stark impossibility of thinking *that*. (1973: xv)

This 'shattering' experience of being confronted with an alien way of thinking and classifying things led Foucault to reconsider what is normally understood as 'the history of ideas', and the way in which we understand our connections with past ages. When we look at the past, and relate it to the present, we usually do so in terms of two main ideas—the search for origins (where we came from, when 'what we are and became' really started) and the notions of progress and development (things are getting better, knowledge is increasing). In the film *2001: A Space Odyssey*, for instance, human development comes about because aliens visit the earth and 'start us off' on the road to civilisation. The recent Steven Spielberg film *Amistad* is another example of this idea—at a particular moment in history it is more or less legally demonstrated that slavery is wrong, and everything (supposedly) changes from that point. With this way of thinking, all the ideas and values that make up our present societies and cultures (individualism, democracy, capitalism) can be identified as having come into being at a certain moment in history; and the only difference between now and, say, four hundred years ago is that our ancestors hadn't worked things out as well, and didn't know as much as we do now.

This idea that the past, rather than being a 'foreign country', is a rough copy of our own place, time and world-view is perpetuated at all levels of our culture. History subjects at school and university are often based on narratives that start with an important event or idea—the Magna Carta, the Battle of Hastings, the culture of ancient Greece—and then show how history unfolded until it reached the present. The signing of the Magna Carta by King John of England, for instance, is put forward as the first big step in the movement from a system of rule based on the divine right of kings to modern parliamentary government. In between, Cromwell's Roundheads had to defeat King Charles' Cavaliers—but it was more or less bound to happen that way, because that's the way 'progress' was moving. The Battle of Hastings 'created' the British nation which after resisting all foreign threats and invasions (from the Spanish, French and Germans) went on to shape the world as we know it today (by 'settling' America, defeating Germany in two world wars, and colonising Africa,

Asia and Australia). And, finally, that everything we in 'the West' consider important today (freedom and democracy, truth and beauty, medicine and science) can be traced back to Athens and Greek culture, and 'names' such as Plato, Hippocrates, Pythagoras and Aristotle.

Much the same thing happens in popular culture. Historical films or television series, whether they are meant to be serious and accurate (such as *I, Claudius*), based around an historical figure (*Braveheart, Rob Roy*), or just an excuse to dress attractive bodies up in short tunics (*Xena, Hercules*), all presume that the people involved are more or less the same as us, and that they share the same outlook on the world. And not just people—words, concepts and ideas are all treated as if they translate easily from one period to another. The way the word 'love', for instance, is used in all of the shows referred to above is pretty much the same. When characters from ancient Rome and Greece or thirteenth-century Scotland say 'I love you', those words are meant to mean exactly what we in the late twentieth century understand by them.

The thing that Foucault reacted to in the Borges story was the idea that people in another time and place may have understood things altogether differently from us—and more than that; they made sense of the world in ways we couldn't possible imagine. What Foucault produced, in *The Order of Things*, was what Michel de Certeau described as 'the history of ideas in Western Europe over the last four hundred years' (1986: 174), but it was a history that didn't find continuity, progress, origins, and that things were 'the same'. Instead, Foucault came up with the notion of periods of history—what he called 'epistemes'—that were organised round their own specific world-views. And the rise and fall of these epistemes didn't correspond to any neat narrative of origins, development, continuity or progress. Just as modern scientists have cast doubt on what has been called the 'teleology' of theories of natural evolution (for instance, the idea that dinosaurs 'had' to die out and give way to mammals, and eventually to human beings), so too Foucault, in *The Order of Things*, challenges the idea that 'what we are' today had to be, or can be, traced back to some original moment, event or culture (such as the Magna Carta, the Battle of Hastings or ancient Greece).

What was supposed to have killed off the dinosaurs was evolution and natural selection—mammals, the story went, were more intelligent, better equipped to handle changing conditions, and generally more advanced. And what was supposed to have driven changing periods and events in human history, supposedly, was not evolution but what is called an historical 'a priori' (such as human reason or, for Marxists, dialectical materialism). Contemporary science now thinks that, rather than being naturally replaced by a higher life form through a steady process of natural selection, the dinosaurs (and millions of other life forms) were killed off by a cataclysmic event such as a meteor hitting the earth, and/or thousands of volcanoes erupting simultaneously, screening off the sun. Foucault argues similarly that epistemes, rather than simply evolving into a different episteme characterised by a higher level of reason, appear and disappear suddenly—and equally arbitrarily.

Epistemes

What does Foucault understand by the term episteme? In some ways it's easier to say what he thinks an episteme is not. It's not a single body of knowledge—our current age, for instance, can't be explained simply in terms of scientific knowledge—or a 'spirit' of the age (for example capitalism or individualism). Nor can the current episteme be understood in terms of the influence of an individual, such as Hitler, Stalin, Mao, Frank Sinatra or Bill Gates. Instead, Foucault refers to an 'order of things' which organises everything, makes some things possible and others impossible, permits us to say some things but makes other things unthinkable. Certeau writes that:

Between the many institutions, experiences, and doctrines of an age, he [Foucault] detects a coherence which, though not explicit, is nonetheless the condition and organizing principle of a culture. There is, therefore, order. But this 'Reason' is a ground that escapes the notice of the very people whose ideas and exchanges it provides the foundation for. No one can express in words that which gives everyone the power to speak. There *is* order, but only in the form of what one does not know. (1986: 172)

In short, an episteme is the product of certain organising principles which relate things to one another (by classifying things, and by allocating them meanings and values) and which, as a result, determines how we make sense of things, what we can know, and what we say. At the same time, these principles are more or less unconscious—we don't go around thinking about them, or referring to them. They are the grounds on which we base everything, so we more or less take them for granted. Certeau explains why it is difficult for us to be aware of or question 'the grounds' of our episteme by referring to cartoons (1986: 183) where a character (say Felix the Cat or Wiley Coyote) is walking on thin air: as long as they don't notice that there is nothing beneath them, they are fine—they keep going—however, as soon as they become aware that they aren't on firm ground(s), they fall into the void.

What are some examples of the way in which an episteme organises thought? Take the idea of medicine. Most people accept, without thinking, that what we call medicine is useful, valuable and good for you. Why? Because all kinds of institutions (hospitals, medical colleges, government bureaucracies, schools, the media) tell us that this is so. But we are also told what 'real' medicine is (say, antibiotics) compared with what it isn't (anti-oxidant vitamins, the blood of a chicken prepared by a witch, or holy water from Lourdes, for example). This 'order of things' is based on the relation between the idea of scientific principles, methods and reason, on the one hand, and a body of practices undertaken by doctors and nurses on the other. Things (people, ideas, materials, approaches) are classified as either medicine—which is valuable and scientific—or as folk remedies or mumbo jumbo which isn't to be taken seriously or treated as if it were valuable. Think of the controversy that erupted in England because Glen Hoddle, the then-national football manager, was sending his players to see a faith healer. There would have been no such controversy if he had sent them to a physiotherapist.

Another example is the way in which life forms are classified. People who have been educated in conventional western thought usually think of life forms in terms of scientific classifications—insects, birds, fish, amphibians, reptiles, lawyers, mammals, that sort of thing. When we come across some life form, this system of classification automatically comes into play and (more or less unconsciously) determines our thinking—that is, determines how we see different creatures. This classificatory system is based on the idea that certain creatures share physical characteristics which constitute 'sameness' (mammals are warm-blooded and suckle their young), and which differentiate them from other creatures (reptiles, amphibians and lawyers are cold-blooded and lay eggs).

If we return to the 'imaginary' classificatory system for animals quoted at the beginning of the chapter we see that it doesn't differentiate animals on the basis of whether they are warm- or cold-blooded, have fur, or suckle their young, but on an entirely different set of principles that are outside our way of thinking. For example, this system separates those animals that have 'just broken the water pitcher', from those that 'belong to the Emperor', have been 'drawn with a very fine camel-hair brush', or 'from a long way off look like flies'. This way of classifying animals couldn't exist in our age because the principles upon which it is based aren't 'scientific' or, to our way of thinking, aren't consistent. After all, they are based on something that has either just happened (breaking the water pitcher), ownership (belonging to the Emperor), means of representation (a camel-hair brush) or on a vague likeness (they look like flies). This, to our minds, is a jumble. But only because the very basis of how we understand 'same'; and 'different' (consistent physical characteristics equal 'same', ownership and means of representation are 'different') is part of, and is given to us by, our episteme. In another time, the idea that 'sameness' could be based purely on shared physical characteristics might be unthinkable—and laughable.

Foucault identifies, on a very general level, three major epistemes which, according to him, have operated over the last four hundred years—the Renaissance, the Classical, and the Modern. None of these are entirely consistent or unchanging, and there is both continuity and discontinuity between them. Now, in some ways this would seem to resemble the notion of 'paradigm shifts' developed by American philosopher Thomas Kuhn. This posits that scientific reason develops in a more or less linear progression, with each paradigm 'discovering' things that the previous, less developed paradigm couldn't understand. In other words, Kuhn suggested that scientific shifts were like building blocks—you built on what was available (on those scientific truths that were already known), and added any new truths to the existing body of knowledge.

Foucault's idea is quite different from this, because he does not see a linear and progressive development from the Renaissance to the Modern age—just examples of sameness and difference. The differences are easy enough to identify. For instance, in the Renaissance, according to Foucault, people understood the world as a kind of book that God had written, and everything (nature, people's behaviour, buildings) could be interpreted in terms of a divine code which had to be deciphered. In fact, Foucault refers to the Renaissance as the 'age of resemblances', because the idea then was that everything resembled (echoed, or imitated) something else, and it was only through God's code that all these resemblances could be fitted together, deciphered and made to make sense. In the Classical age, with the rise of scientific approaches, the world came to be understood in terms of natural order. Various things, they thought, could be identified through careful observation, and understood through the use of 'tables of measurement'. That is, people began to understand and articulate things by pulling them out of their 'isolation', comparing one thing with another, and then arranging them in a table from the simplest to the most complex. The Modern age is different again because, whereas previously the order of things could be traced back to either God or Nature, now 'man' is responsible for knowledge. So the 'measure of all things' from the end of the eighteenth century, according to Foucault, was not God or Nature, but 'man'.

Of course there is also continuity and sameness across epistemes, but for Foucault the sameness is actually an illusion based on misinterpretations. Certeau gives the following comment and example:

> On one level, we have a surface permanence which,
> despite shiftings of ground, keeps words, concepts,
> or symbolic themes the same. A simple example: the
> 'madman' is spoken of in the sixteenth, eighteenth and
> nineteenth centuries, but actually 'it is not a question of
> the *same* malady' in any two of them. The same thing
> applies to theological exegesis as it does to medicine. The
> same words do not designate the same things. Ideas,
> themes, classifications float from one mental universe
> to another, but at each passage they are affected by
> structures which reorganize them and endow them
> with a new meaning. The same mental objects 'function'
> differently . . . Thus the fear which in the sixteenth
> century exiled the madman in an effort to avoid diabolical
> contagion, in the eighteenth century adopts medical
> terminology and resurfaces in the form of precautions
> against the contaminated air of the hospitals. (1986: 179–80)

Certeau's point is that the term 'the madman' has been carried forward from the Renaissance through the Classical age to modernity, but what we now understand by it (and how we treat 'the condition' which is, of course, tied up with ideas derived from contemporary psychology or psychiatry) no longer corresponds to the 'madman' of the Renaissance, whose behaviour would have been understood as an effect of the moon or having been possessed by the devil. Although medical science is usually understood as a discipline based on the development, clarification and progression of scientific knowledge (the idea being that we learn more about things and become better at dealing with them as time goes on), Foucault argues that there is no necessary connection between periods: that there is no natural linkage between, and movement from, one episteme to another. Remember the examples referred to earlier in this chapter—the Magna Carta, the Battle of Hastings, and ancient Greece. All of these are understood today as being part of the origins of the present: as events, moments or ideas which began a movement which not only produced democracy, the western world and high culture respectively, but which also could move only forward, inexorably and in an essential form, to the present.

Let's now return to the analogy of the extinction of the dinosaurs. Darwin's theory of evolution more or less claims that the dinosaurs had to die out because there were superior life forms ready to replace them. In this scenario, the movement of life is towards the ultimate life form—humanity. Much the same idea is behind theories of the 'inevitable progression' of civilisation—that there is an ideal, ultimate and complete form of civilisation, and that humanity is developing steadily and inevitably towards that point. What Foucault does is to suggest that what we have, think, know and understand today was not inevitable but, because of the way in which our episteme is ordered, we have very little chance of either understanding that things could have been different, or of speaking differently about them. The question is, how do epistemes 'speak themselves', and exclude everything else?

Discursive formations

In *The Archaeology of Knowledge* Foucault tries to show how epistemes work and 'speak themselves' through what he calls the production of 'discursive formations', or 'orders of discourse'. Discursive formations are the organising principles of an episteme. They work to make speech possible, organise ideas or concepts, and produce 'objects of knowledge'. For an example of this we will turn again to the 'madman' and the notion of insanity. In our contemporary society, what comes to be designated as madness, how it is described, and what is done about it (a process we could call 'the discursive production of madness') depends on three major factors— what Foucault has identified, in a more general context, as disciplines, commentary, and the author.

In our culture, madness is very much 'owned' by disciplines such as psychology, psychoanalysis and psychiatry. These disciplines, and the institutions, discourses and practitioners associated with them, more or less have the task of having the final word on madness. If someone's behaviour is being evaluated or judged in a court of law, for instance, the court will rely upon these disciplines (say, in the form of expert witnesses) to guide their decision. Those experts get their expertise and knowledge by becoming familiar with the discourses and texts (books, articles, conference papers, policy documents, case studies) that provide commentary on, and in the process end up producing, the 'object of madness'. In order to become a fully accredited practitioner in these disciplines, individuals must negotiate the various institutional hurdles (a relevant degree, for instance) which continually test their 'fit' with the discourses, logics and ways of thinking of that particular discipline.

Much of what is accepted as legitimate disciplinary knowledge depends on, and is organised around, 'names'. If you were doing a subject in psychoanalysis at university, for instance, everything would be organised around the work of authors such as Freud, Jung, Adler, Jones, Reich, Klein and Lacan. These 'names' hold a privileged place in the discipline—the commentaries and theories they produce carry what the French sociologist Pierre Bourdieu calls 'cultural capital', and practitioners continually reinterpret their works, providing commentaries on commentaries *ad infinitum*. Whether an act or a person is considered mad on not might depend on which 'expert' carried the most capital, or on which group of practitioners a government consulted when it drew up its policies.

This combination of disciplines, commentary and authors constitutes a kind of machine which produces the so-called 'truth of madness' which edits out and condemns anything that doesn't fit within the 'discursive formation' at either a local (discipline-based) or general (culture-based) level. If a practitioner were suddenly to decide that madness really was a kind of demonic possession, and to suggest that patients be subjected to exorcisms, as was considered perfectly reasonable four hundred years ago, that person would automatically disqualify themselves from any claims to be a legitimate member of the discipline, because the 'order of reason' they were working out of belonged to a previous time.

We can see, in this example of discursive formations, just how epistemes are the 'same but different'. During the Renaissance, people might be designated 'possessed' if their hair was sticking up on either side of their heads in the shape of two little horns—just like the devil. Remember, that episteme, according to Foucault, was based on the logic of the 'truth of resemblance'. There is a comic example of this other 'order of things' in the film *Monty Python and the Search for the Holy Grail*, when a group of villagers is trying to decide if a woman is a witch. A 'knowledgeable' person explains how they can work things out: 'we burn witches, so they must be made of wood; wood floats in water; ducks also float in water; so, if the woman weighs the same as a duck, she must be a witch'. Strangely enough, it works—'It's a fair cop', she says.

In our time, you wouldn't be arrested or institutionalised for looking like the devil, or because you weighed the same as a duck, but you are analysed and read (within the family, at school and church, in hospitals) in terms of signs that point to your 'truth'. One of the organising principles of our age, for instance, is the notion of the 'unconscious', or the idea that beneath the surface of events and things can be found the 'real' truth. When serial killers or mass murderers are identified, for instance, they are scrutinised, analysed and scientifised to death (particularly in the media) in search of

23

signs that should have alerted us to what they were really like (and which can be used to identify potential deviants). In both cases (being possessed by the devil, and being a mass murderer) the process looks the same (you read the signs to discover 'the truth'), but the logic that is behind the readings is very different—one is based on a divine order of resemblances, the other is based on various forms of science.

Genealogy

Foucault became particularly interested in what the German philosopher Nietzsche called 'genealogy'. Genealogy, for Nietzsche, involved investigating the historical origins of powerful institutions and discourses which claimed to be universal and eternal. The best-known example that Nietzsche refers to is Christianity. Nietzsche argues that Christian morality (based on the notion that 'the meek shall inherit the earth') came about because Christians were 'the meek' (they were oppressed by the Romans), and they were just making up stories about how, one day, everything would be different. So instead of being 'for all time', Christian morality, for Nietzsche, arose out of, and was all about, a specific historical context.

Foucault's genealogies work in the same way. Whereas his 'archaeological' work concentrated on 'attempting to mark out and distinguish the principles of ordering . . . and exclusion' (Rabinow 1986: 105) that made discursive formations and epistemes possible, in subsequent books (such as *Discipline and Punish* and the first volume of *The History of Sexuality*) he took issue with two of the most important and unquestioned concepts of our modern age—the notion that truth could be identified in a disinterested way and, relatedly, that knowledge was something that was independent of power.

We tend to think of truth and knowledge as forming the basis of our society and culture—they are the grounds on which we walk. But Foucault suggests that, like everything else, they have a history—one which is closely related to the way in which operations and relations of power have been transformed over the last four hundred years. He argues that prior to the seventeenth century:

> . . . the mode in which power was exercised could be defined in its essentials in terms of the relationship sovereign-subject. But in the seventeenth and eighteenth centuries, we have the production of an important phenomenon, the emergence, or rather the invention, of a new mechanism of power. (Foucault 1980: 104)

Whereas at one point in history power could be understood quite simply in terms of a king or queen having a divine right to exercise it (they more or less stood in for God, so you couldn't really argue with them), from the seventeenth century on that guarantor of power—God—was replaced by something else—truth and knowledge. Remember we pointed out earlier that the order of 'divine resemblances' that characterised the Renaissance was replaced by two very different orders—one (the Classical age) based on the 'truth of nature', and the other (modernity) based on 'man'. The most important aspect of these transformations was the development of what Foucault calls 'the human sciences', which comprise those disciplines which purport to scientifically produce knowledge of, and the truth about, people. In *The History of Sexuality*, for instance, Foucault demonstrates how the nineteenth century, which is normally thought of as being very puritanical ('the Victorian age'), and silent with regard to sex, was in fact characterised by institutions and disciplines producing vast amounts of knowledge about sex, which supposedly gave us access to the truth about people. It did this by moving from knowledge, which was collected from observations, accounts, testimonies, confessions, to the truth— think of categories, such as the homosexual, the frigid woman, the accountant, the nymphomaniac or the hysteric, that have passed into everyday language. These categories and their symptoms became established as 'conditions' which distinguished 'normal and healthy' people from 'deviants and perverts', and which could be treated (by surgery, electric shocks, therapy, analysis).

These forms of knowledge were concentrated in the medical sciences (including discipline areas such as psychiatry and psychology) which made use of scientific principles, such as observation, testing, experimentation and analysis to produce classifications and categories of human sexuality and sexual behaviour. Perhaps the most interesting development in the early twentieth century was in the areas of psychology and psychoanalysis which, through theorists such as Freud, claimed to have discovered virtually a new world of human experience. Narratives, categories, terms and explanations (the Oedipal complex, the unconscious, the ego, super-ego, ego-ideal, sublimation) more or less rewrote the script (the 'truth') not only of the human psyche, but of everyday life and behaviour as well—think of Freudian slips, the notion of unconscious repression, and the way in which our repressed desires are supposedly played out in our dreams.

Foucault argued that the knowledge and truth produced by the human sciences was, on one level, tied to power because of the way in which it was used to regulate and normalise individuals. Remember we made the point earlier that 'madness' doesn't just exist—it is produced by disciplinary knowledge. The state drafts policies and laws that determine legally who is normal and healthy, and who is morally or physically perverted and dangerous. However, those policies and laws are based on the knowledge produced by disciplines and institutions. In other words, knowledge, in a sense, authorises and legitimates the exercising of power.

Foucault suggests, following Nietzsche, that truth and knowledge are tied up with power in another way. We mentioned before that our age identifies certain points of origin from which its most important ideas and values can be traced (democracy from the Magna Carta, the idea of the West from the Battle of Hastings, beauty and high culture from ancient Greece). But Foucault shows that such claims are illusory— that there never was any essential connection between events and ideas across different epistemes. Why make such claims, then? Because, as both Nietzsche and Foucault point out, dominant disciplines and discourses are not simply the new guarantors of power—replacing God—their development, and the knowledge and truth that they produce, are the result of power struggles in which they have triumphed over other disciplines and forms of knowledge. Nietzsche once suggested that where there is meaning, it is possible to trace the struggles, battles and violence that produced it. Part of the tactics of such struggles is to claim a universal and eternal truth for your discipline and knowledge—because that's a pretty reasonable position of strength to be arguing from. To do that, you have to demonstrate, or argue for, the connections between your discipline and its antecedents. For example, Freud claimed that many of his insights could be found in, and traced back to, ancient Greek culture—hence the Oedipal complex.

Let's stay with psychology and psychoanalysis for a relatively recent example of the way in which the 'truth of knowledge' can be shown to be the result of cultural and institutional struggles. In his essay 'Psychoanalysis and its History' (1986), Michel de Certeau recounts a quite extraordinary story about the field(s) of psychology/psychoanalysis and the power struggles that characterised them after the death of Freud—a story which seems to echo the narrative Freud himself produced in *Totem and Taboo*. In that book, Freud theorises that the taboos and prohibitions that have existed in cultures from time immemorial can be traced back to an original time and event (Nietzsche would be smiling here) when a group of sons who made up a tribe rebelled against and killed their father, who had sole sexual access to the tribe's women. After killing their father, the sons felt extremely guilty, and so transformed the dead father into an authority figure (a kind of God)—who ended up more or less ruling the tribe from the grave.

Certeau argues that something similar happened with Freud and the field(s) associated with his work. While he was alive, his work and theories were challenged by many of his colleagues (Certeau writes of his 'sons' Adler and Jung) in different countries (he was rejected in France because of the opposition of powerful institutions such as the 'Paris School of Psychology and Psychiatry'). After his death, however, he became a kind of god, and battles raged around the world about who the real heirs of Freud were, and what his works really meant. Again, Nietzsche's point about origins is very important here. Practitioners in a discipline such as psychoanalysis attempt to make connections between the discourses and work that they are producing, and the 'founder' of the discipline, because such connections authorise their version of events—and further their careers.

Conclusion

In this chapter we have suggested that Foucault's notions of the order of things and epistemes constituted a new way of looking at what is usually referred to as 'the history of ideas'. Our age (what Foucault calls 'modernity') thinks of itself as the heir to a long tradition of ideas, values, principles and practices going back thousands of years. Politicians, university lecturers, school teachers, civil servants, business people and artists all trace their beliefs and values and activities back to certain moments in history in order to show their enduring value and universality. The English Renaissance writer Ben Jonson, in eulogising Shakespeare, said that he was 'not of a time, but of all time'—the point being that, while lesser writers might be appreciated for a while, Shakespeare would 'speak' to everyone across the ages. Politicians make the same kind of claim when they talk about the 'need to protect the precious flame of democracy which has been burning since the days of ancient Greece'. These two examples can be understood as being claims about 'sameness'—Shakespeare's works, and the form of democracy that emerged in ancient Greece, are both supposedly connected to us because they see the world pretty much as we see it today. The main points we can take from this are:

- Foucault's concept of epistemes—periods of history organised around, and explicable in terms of, specific world-views and discourses—shows that the way in which people make sense of their world depends on an order of reason and sets of discursive formations that do not translate from one to another;
- There can still be continuities from one episteme to the other—for instance, we still read and value Shakespeare, and think that democracy is important. But Foucault's point is that we think Shakespeare and democracy are essentially what we make of them, and we project that 'essence' back onto other epistemes, ideas and events. The knowledge that is produced in our episteme is also our 'truth'—and it ends up becoming everybody else's 'truth' as well;
- Knowledge and truth are not essential and ahistorical, but are produced by epistemes and, at the same time, hold that episteme together. What this means is that knowledge and truth are tied up with the way in which power is exercised in our age (as, for instance, governments use the human sciences to help frame laws and policies), and are themselves caught up in power struggles.

Further reading

Certeau, Michel de 1984, *The Practice of Everyday Life*, University of California Press, Berkeley, see Chapter 4
——1986, *Heterologies: Discourse on the Other*, University of Minnesota Press, Minneapolis, see Chapter 12
McNay, Lois 1994, *Foucault: A Critical Introduction*, Continuum, New York, see Chapter 12

3

Discourses and institutions

People in contemporary western societies think of themselves very much as individuals—they tend to think that they are in charge of their lives, that they make their own meanings and that, through a process of development and learning, they are able to reflect upon experiences and make sense of them. It is this faculty that is supposed to distinguish us from animals, and those 'less fortunate' individuals who, because of mental incapacity or distress or because they have been classified as holding 'primitive' world-views, are not able to govern, or reason their way through, their thoughts and actions in the 'western' way.

This idea of the self-knowing, individual subject in control of his or her thoughts and actions permeates our culture to such an extent that we never really question it. Contemporary popular culture provides plenty of examples of how this idea is both reinforced and valued. Think of any contemporary film hero or heroine—Harrison Ford fighting terrorists in *Patriot Games* or *Clear and Present Danger*, Sigourney Weaver up against aliens and the company in the *Alien* films, or the whole *Star Trek* crew in their battles with the Borg: in all these examples the 'good guys' are individuals who think for themselves, reason things out, and make decisions. This supposedly distinguishes them from terrorists, aliens and cyborgs, all of whom are driven by something (fanatical political beliefs, instinct, programming) over which they have no control.

Foucault rejects this idea of the self-governing subject, pointing out that what comes between ourselves and our experience is the grounds upon which we can act, speak and make sense of things. For Foucault, one of the most significant forces shaping our experiences is language. Try coming up with a thought, or making sense of an experience, without using language to do so. We not only use language to explain our ideas and feelings to others, we use it to explain things to ourselves. Foucault is not so much interested in language systems as a whole, as in individual acts of language—or discourse. Discourses can be understood as language in action: they are the windows, if you like, which allow us to make sense of, and 'see' things. These discursive windows or explanations shape our understanding of ourselves, and our capacity to distinguish the valuable from the valueless, the true from the false, and the right from the wrong.

For Foucault, while we are not just programmed or driven by instinct, our thoughts and actions are influenced, regulated and to some extent controlled by these different discourses. A good example is in the first *Alien* film, where the crew have been taught to unthinkingly identify with, and serve, the company and its discourses, values and ways of doing things (putting profit, productivity, and economic rationalism above human life). They think that they are acting as free individuals, but it is only when it becomes clear that the company thinks that they are expendable do they start to question what has been happening to them.

Some writers have attacked Foucault for his rejection of the idea of a self-governing subject. For example, the art critic and historian Robert Hughes argues that Foucault's ideas suggest that 'we are not in control of our own history and never can be' (1993: 71). He contrasts significant political events, such as the Tiananmen Square massacre in Beijing in

1989, with what he regards as the theoretical dead end produced through Foucault's thought:

> In the late 1980s, while American academics were emptily theorising that truth, language and the thinking subject were dead, the longing for freedom and humanistic culture were demolishing the very pillars of European tyranny. Of course, if the Chinese students had read their Foucault they would have known that repression is inscribed in all language, their own included, and so they could have saved themselves the trouble of facing the tanks in Tiananmen Square. (1993: 72)

In this passage Hughes uses words such as 'truth', 'freedom', and 'tyranny' in an unqualified manner. He assumes that everybody will understand and agree on what these terms mean. In Hughes' writing, these terms are assumed to be fundamental values of a society whose meaning is fixed for everyone and for all time. Foucault, in contrast, writes about relations of power, domains of knowledge, games of truth, forms of subjectivity, techniques of the self and orders of discourse. In each of these cases, the first term is at least as important as the second because, as was discussed in the previous chapter, it is the particular relations, domains, games, forms, techniques and orders of a social context that shape the kind of power, knowledge, truth, subjectivity, self, and discourse that apply within that context.

We can return later to Robert Hughes' argument that what Foucault is suggesting is that human beings can never be in control of their history or destiny. In this chapter we will work through the implications of Foucault's ideas on discourse and institutions, drawing particularly from his book, *The Archaeology of Knowledge*.

Discourse and field

The relationships between people and their experiences, and the grounds which they occupy, comprise various social and cultural fields, such as education, politics, science or sport. We can think of a field as a piece of territory, or a space within society, that gets used in particular ways. Each field lays down rules and procedures, assigns roles and positions, regulates behaviours and what can be said, and produces hierarchies. For example, the field of politics has procedures for running parliamentary sessions, assigns roles such as politician and administrator, deems certain behaviours or forms of language inappropriate (think of the Bill Clinton sex case in the late 1990s), and produces a hierarchy that means certain positions carry greater authority than others.

It's important to recognise that the roles within the field precede the people who occupy these roles. There has been a president of the United States of America since the eighteenth century—Bill Clinton has only occupied that role since 1993. So, in assuming a position within a field, the person enters into the processes which regulate what occurs within the field, and their identity or subjectivity is shaped by the operations of that field. Think back to the example from the film *Alien*— the crew were, in a sense, the products of their field, and the discourses and values that characterised it. They treated the universe as if it were a giant resource to be mined by the company—everything, as far as their field was concerned, was a means to an end, and the end was to increase the wealth and power of the company, and make its employees (themselves) rich. It's only when they are defined as means (their lives are to be sacrificed in order to capture the alien) that they break free of the control of their field and its discourses.

Discourse, as the means through which the field 'speaks' of itself to itself, plays a major role in the operations of the field. So, in mapping out a discursive field, Foucault wants to trace where particular instances of discourse have occurred, to make connections between these instances, and to bring them together to identify a particular discursive formation. These discourses can be found in a variety of sites—government records, books, a person's private correspondence or oral memory.

Discourse and events

Foucault emphasises that a discourse can also be understood as a series of events. Discursive practices occur at a particular time, and are like events in that they create effects within a discursive field. An example could be something as mundane as records documenting the movement of ships into and out of a particular harbour over a 50-year period. A study of such records might find that, from a certain time, references to piracy began to crop up—or to enter the discourse. What such references would show is that piracy had become a problem for that harbour's shipping authorities. It may have been the case that acts of piracy had occurred previously, but it is not until it enters the discourse of those records that it has a status within the practices and concerns of the shipping authorities. Certain events may have occurred quite regularly—ships attacked, people killed, and goods stolen by men with wooden legs and parrots on their shoulders—but until these things were recognised as constituting something called 'piracy', they would have been ignored, and given some other discursive explanation (say, rebellion, or acts of war, or just wild Friday nights).

We can find a more recent example in the meteorological discourse used in weather bulletins. During the 1990s there was an increase in references to things like global warming, or the El Niño weather pattern that disrupts 'normal' weather patterns, changing rainfall and temperature levels in the affected areas. These references are discursive events which have such an impact that they do not simply affect meteorological practice, but actually create effects in other fields such as politics (politicians blame El Niño for not delivering on their promises) and economics (governments change economic policies, and markets rise or fall, depending on the idea of the 'El Niño effect'). In the United States in the late 1990s, a person became so upset by this El Niño business that he looked up the phone book, found somebody called El Niño, and went over and shot him.

Discourses, statements and discursive formations

The basic unit of discourse is the statement. For Foucault, discourses are made up of statements that set up relationships with other statements: they share a space and establish contexts; they may also disappear and be replaced by other statements. Statements are essentially rare because, while a discourse can potentially take in an indefinite number of statements, usually only a limited number actually constitutes any discourse, and these are referred to again and again.

The field of law, for example, has a limited set of statements which establish the conditions for the truth upon which it arbitrates and makes judgements. A good example of this is the situation of sexual harrassment. In the 1980s Professor Anita Hill claimed that she had been sexually harrassed, years earlier, by Judge Clarence Thomas, who was about to be appointed to the US Supreme Court. Many people criticised Hill for waiting so long to say anything: 'Why,' they asked, 'didn't she make a complaint when this thing happened?' The answer she gave was quite simple: sexual harrassment didn't actually 'exist' (in a legal sense) at the time she was working for Thomas. We could say that prior to the Hill–Thomas affair, legal and social relationships in the United States were organised around a statement about gender relations—say, to the effect that 'woman are not full subjects, like men'—which allowed, and more or less encouraged, men to impose themselves sexually on woman. This is why other forms of violence, such as rape within marriage, didn't really 'exist' either (at least as discursive realities). Of course once this statement ceased to determine things (though in fact it still functions in most cultures), all kinds of violence suddenly became visible, and changed the way in which people could relate to, and treat, one another. In other words, the questioning and challenging of the statement brought about changes to different discursive formations (domestic, legal, bureaucratic, political).

Discursive formations are defined as much by what lies outside them as what lies within. Take science as an example of a discursive formation: since the sixteenth century, science has moved into more and more areas of experience, taking in the sciences of life (biology and medicine), the physical sciences (physics, chemistry), and the human or social sciences (economics, psychology, sociology). Each of these domains can be identified as a science because they have certain common principles for evaluating truth and regulating practices within their fields—for instance, methods of verification, falsification, experimentation, analysis and argumentation.

The discursive formation of science is also defined in relation to areas that it doesn't take in; those from which it distinguishes itself. These 'others' will vary according to shifts across time. For example, in the Middle Ages, the 'other' of science was witchcraft or sorcery. In the Age of Enlightenment, the 'other' tended to be religious doctrine. More recently, 'New Age' mysticism is generally distinguished as the 'other' of science. But it can be the case that an area which at one time lies outside science subsequently crosses the scientific threshold, and becomes incorporated into it. The increasing 'scientific legitimacy' granted to areas such as naturopathy and herbal remedies is evidence of this trend.

Foucault describes this part of his work as archival and archaeological. Just as an archaeologist digs through various layers of soil and rock to uncover the various objects from different historical societies that have accumulated within a site, Foucault's archaeology involves working through the historical archives of various societies to bring to light the discursive formations and events that have created the fields of knowledge and games of truth by which that society has governed itself.

Institutions

Foucault's work on discourse has implications for understanding the operations of institutions. We can define an institution as a relatively enduring and stable set of relationships between different people, and between people and objects. For instance, the field of education is made up of a variety of institutions: schools, universities, kindergartens, and bureaucracies. These institutions invariably have a physical presence—for example, a classroom—but, importantly, they should also be understood as being constituted by relationships: between school principals and teachers, teachers and students, parents and school boards, and so on.

Institutions can be found across the various fields into which society is divided: educational, legal, penal, business, governmental, family, sporting, recreational, religious, cultural. These institutions have been characterised as belonging to either the private sphere (of family and personal concerns) or the public sphere (of work, economics, government, education and so forth). The public sphere is generally more institutionalised and regulated than the private. For example, there seems to be a relatively fixed and rigid set of protocols and procedures for regulating communication practices in public sphere institutions such as the law and big business, while a private sphere concern such as love or friendship seems much less rigid. It would be quite acceptable to address a close friend or lover by some 'pet' name such as 'honeybun' or 'brave beaver'; it would be courting disaster to address a judge or managing director in such terms.

For Foucault these differences between public and private institutions are tied up with the notions of truth and 'truth effects'. Public institutions draw their authority from their capacity to speak the truth about some situation. Legal institutions deliver the truth in their deliberations on criminal cases; scientific institutions pronounce the truth about breakthroughs in knowledge; government institutions are supposed to make judgements about the true and best way to administer society. Of course private institutions, like families, also 'speak the truth'. In reminiscing over a holiday held ten years ago, for instance, family members will often carefully recount details, argue over the accuracy of their relatives' memories, and finally pronounce the truth of the holiday—where we went, what we did, who we saw, whether we had fun. The difference between the truths of the private and the public institutions is that the public truths have far wider effects across society.

Of course, it might be pointed out that public institutions regularly fail in their role as guardians of the truth. Judges have been known to convict innocent people, as in the Guildford Four case in Britain which was the subject of the film *In the Name of the Father*, where the British legal system (including the police and judges) quite literally manufactured the truth to get certain people convicted. And science makes what are often dramatic mistakes, as in the disastrous use of Thalidomide in the 1950s to combat morning sickness which resulted in malformed babies. In fact, Foucault has argued that scientific discoveries emerge less from a disinterested quest for the absolute truth about the world, and more as a result of chance encounters, institutional politics and practices of patronage and favouritism. For example, there will be an economic incentive for scientists to produce improvements in the efficiency of weapons of mass destruction (the arms industry is one of the biggest in the world); there will be considerably less economic support to find more environmentally friendly fuel sources (indeed, large oil companies have resisted such a move).

The Bill Clinton affair

The point Foucault emphasises is that, even though public institutions often fail to uphold their values of truth, it is these values upon which they are judged. An example is the Bill Clinton sex scandal which led to his impeachment trial in early 1999. The basis of the move for impeachment was not so much that the president had committed adultery. Two far more 'scandalous' issues were at stake: first, those bringing the charges accused him of having misled the nation on the details of that affair; and second, those encounters were supposed to have taken place near the Oval Office in the White House.

These two issues are, of course, closely connected. Presidents ought not to mislead the nation, because the high office of president is supposed to represent values of absolute integrity, honesty and justice. And critically, the president ought not to have committed adultery in the Oval Office, because that office, as the literal embodiment of the presidential role, is also understood to embody presidential values—to be a place of integrity, honesty and justice. Former president Ronald Reagan is reported to have always donned a jacket before entering this inner sanctum. So the Oval Office requires that people put on clothes rather than remove them, because—as with the king's costume referred to previously—clothing and finery contribute to the authority of a position. And while it is acceptable to utilise the Oval Office to make military decisions that might lead to the deaths of millions of people, it is not acceptable to engage in sexual relations there.

The Clinton case is also interesting from a Foucaultian perspective because it indicates that something is, in a sense, not true, and indeed does not exist, until it is articulated through discourse. For example, Clinton is not the first president to engage in extramarital sexual activities in the White House. But this was the first time a president's extramarital affair had become the subject of considerable discourse. The volume of discourse increased exponentially as the case unfolded throughout 1998. It became the subject of the Starr Report (legal discourse—the report by investigator Kenneth Starr into whether the president had lied under oath about his relationship with his intern, Monica Lewinsky); it impacted on political and economic issues (political and economic discourse); and, of course, it had exhaustive press and television coverage (media discourse). This confirms Foucault's point that something doesn't become a problem, or have a problematic status, until it enters into a discourse.

While considerable discursive effort was expended within various fields to work through the implications of Clinton's affairs, it is believed that the sheer volume of the discourse, and the areas into which this discourse moved (involving speculation about the presidential penis and sex acts involving cigars) was instrumental in alienating people from the case.

It is significant that the public reacted against the discourse (its volume and the areas it covered) rather than against the actions of the man who had brought the discourse into being. There was much less support for impeachment proceedings from the populace than there was from the president's political opponents, a situation that influenced the outcomes of both the American congressional elections in November 1998 and the impeachment trial in 1999.

Games of truth

Foucault uses the term 'games of truth' to emphasise that, while public institutions authorise their activities by claiming to be speaking the truth, these truth claims are dependent on institutional and discursive practices. Foucault defines a game of truth as 'a set of procedures that lead to a certain result, which, on the basis of its principles and rules of procedures, may be considered valid or invalid', or more simply as 'a set of rules by which truth is produced' (1997: 297).

Games of truth are important because they help produce our subjectivity, discursively positioning us to see the truth about ourselves, our desires, and our experiences. And we can find them in both public and private institutions, but the rules by which these games are played out in private institutions such as the family are different from those in public institutions. For instance, family rules involve issues of each partner's affection for and faithfulness towards the other, the duty to bring up children in a particular way, and a responsibility towards extended family members (such as parents and grandparents). These rules are not written down anywhere, but they are real in that they determine or influence how people see themselves and behave. Steven Spielberg's 1998 film *Saving Private Ryan* tells the story of a decision, by Second World War American military command, to send home an American soldier fighting in Europe because his three brothers have all been killed in action, and his family needs a survivor. A group of American soldiers are detailed to find this young man, Private Ryan, and risk their lives to get him—one of their 'family'—back. Now of course there is or was no law, in the army or in general society, about sacrificing yourself for others, but in a sense what the soldiers understood as the 'truth' about themselves depended on notions of loyalty and sacrifice. This explains those occasions when people say something like 'I couldn't live with myself if I let that happen'—they wouldn't want to be themselves if they lost the 'truth' of their character.

We can recognise that, in various forms and through various means, the quest for truth has become fundamental in contemporary western societies. Among other areas, it is found in educational disciplines such as science and history, and in legal and governmental institutions. It is also found in everyday culture, such as television talk shows and popular magazines, where the 'truth' about a celebrity's private life might be revealed, or we might be granted 'beauty secrets' which are meant to reveal the true and correct way in which to appear attractive. As Foucault comments:

> In societies like ours, the 'political economy' of truth is characterized by five important traits. 'Truth' is centered on the form of scientific discourse and the institutions which produce it; it is subject to constant economic and political incitement (the demand for truth, as much for economic power as for political power); it is the object, under diverse forms, of immense diffusion and consumption (circulating through apparatuses of education and information whose extent is relatively broad in the social body, notwithstanding certain strict limitations); it is produced and transmitted under the control, dominant if not exclusive, of a few great political and economic apparatuses (university, army, writing, media); lastly, it is the issue of a whole political debate and social confrontation ('ideological' struggles). (1984b: 73)

Of course, this interest in truth is not unique to contemporary society—as the religious genre of the confession indicates, it has been a fundamental part of the history of Christianity in the West. Foucault's point is to problematise the question of truth, and to show the extent to which it is an effect of the work of discourses and institutions, rather than being absolute or essential.

Discursive flows—private into public

Within contemporary western societies, the media play a particularly significant role in determining what truth is, and make sure that it is valued and 'protected'—for instance, by protecting the public interest from the abuses of power of various public institutions. One of the best-known cases was the instrumental part played by *Washington Post* journalists Carl Bernstein and Bob Woodward in exposing the Watergate cover-up and bringing down the presidency of Richard Nixon in 1974. But, as we saw in the Clinton case, the media is not always consistent in deciding what should become a 'discursive eruption' or a 'media event'. The first rumours about Clinton's relationship with Monica Lewinsky appeared not in 'respectable' publications like the *New York Times* or the *Washington Post*, but on the Internet. This, presumably, wasn't because the 'respectable' newspapers hadn't heard the rumours, but because they had decided initially that rumours of the Lewinsky affair were not fit for publication. In this, the 'respectable' established media were making judgements about what gets constituted as an act of discourse, or a discursive event. This brings into focus the media's conventional watch-dog role as a public institution committed to an examination of other public institutions, to interrogating their truth claims and exposing their deceits. What we see is not a disinterested public watch-dog, but an institution whose own truth claims are based on effectively evaluating the games of truth played out in government, business, education and so on.

While the media's role has conventionally been to make public institutional practices known to readers and viewers within the private sphere of family and home, the media in western societies have increasingly turned their attention to private sphere concerns. For example, the emergence of the 'miracle' drug Viagra—a 'cure' for sexual impotence—became a prominent discursive event, as do the private lives and affairs of an increasing number of politicians, film stars and royalty. Some commentators see this as a trivialising of the media, an abandoning of the principles that gave it its value as a democratic force within modern western societies. More positively, from a Foucaultian perspective, the trend might be seen as producing an awareness of how people's subjectivity is constructed from within the flow of discourse.

An example of how discursive flows create public figures in terms of their private lives is Diana, the late Princess of Wales. The overwhelming majority of people who mourned Diana's death in 1997 had never personally met her. For them, her personality and body image was a complex of various discourses: family life, royalty, romance, physical beauty, the media, mythology and madness (as expressed in the articles that suggested she was unbalanced and prone to paranoia). Two diametrically opposed views situated Diana with regard to these discourses. The first was that she was the innocent victim of hostile forces (the British monarchy and the media) who contributed to her death; the second was that she manipulated these institutions in order to gain advantages for herself.

Perhaps these positions are not so opposed as they first seem. It could be that Diana, conscious of the sheer amount of media discourse devoted to her, did intervene in this discursive construction. Her appearance on the BBC *Panorama* programme in 1995, in which she revealed the extent of her marriage difficulties and her sense of betrayal, is an example of such an intervention. There is a connection between such intervention and Foucault's point that, if we abandon the idea that the sovereign subject is the origin of meaning, we are better able to grasp how our identities are played out within the complex ensembles and discursive flows that produce a multiplicity of subject positions. In Diana's case, these subject positions and personae included 'the people's princess', mother, betrayed wife, and fashion icon.

The public is also able to intervene in the discursive flows through which public figures are constructed. In so doing, they contribute to the making of their own subjectivities. The outpouring of grief in response to Diana's death and funeral is an example. This public grief forced changes in the protocols and procedures of the British monarchy, as shown by the Queen's televised address on the eve of the funeral. It's also notable how the crowds outside Westminster Abbey who watched the service on giant video screens responded to Earl Spencer's eulogy with spontaneous applause which the mourners inside the Abbey heard and took up. The media images of a public service created a feedback loop which then shaped the conduct of that service.

At this point we might return to the objections to Foucault's ideas raised by Robert Hughes. As we saw earlier in this chapter, Hughes is dismissive of Foucault because he reads Foucault as arguing that people can't be in control of their own destinies. And, if this is the case—if our subjectivity is situated within, and transformed by, discursive flows, institutional practices and games of truth, rather than being the product of our conscious, self-governing self—how can we gain some control over ourselves, let alone attempt to shape these social and historical forces?

It is here that Foucault brings in the concepts of thought, criticism and problematisation as ways in which we can both reflect on our own position as social subjects, and attempt to negotiate, and negotiate with, the social order. Thought, for Foucault, is that which allows us to step back from our conduct and to reflect on what we do, on the conditions under which we come to act or react in particular ways, and on what effects this conduct might have. As he writes: 'Thought is freedom in relation to what one does, the motion by which one detaches oneself from it, establishes it as an object, and reflects on it as a problem' (1997: xxxv). This means that, for Foucault, thought is what provides us with the tools for ethical behaviour.

Similarly, he argues that criticism is the critical work we do upon ourselves in order to 'make' our subjectivity as an object of self-reflexive thought. Criticism in this sense is 'a historical investigation into the events that have led us to constitute ourselves and to recognise ourselves as subjects of what we are doing, thinking, saying' (1997: xxxv). Thought and criticism, then, enable us to problematise—and, potentially, transform—our subjectivity.

Conclusion

In this chapter we have discussed Foucault's ideas about discourses and institutions, focusing on how discourses:

- operate as forms of language working through various institutional settings to lay down the grounds upon which we make sense of the world;
- can be analysed at various levels, from their basic constituents, statements, to accumulated discursive formations, which provide the basis for the way in which people make sense of the world in certain times in certain places;
- are associated with 'games of truth', working within fields such as science and government to authorise what can be judged as true or untrue.

Further reading

Best, Steven and Kellner, Douglas 1991, *Postmodern Theory: Critical Interrogations*, Macmillan, London
Deleuze, Gilles 1988, *Foucault*, Athlone Press, London, see 'Strata or historical formations: the visible and the articulable'
Foucault, Michel 1972, *The Archaeology of Knowledge*, Pantheon Books, New York, see 'Appendix: Discourse on language'
McNay, Lois 1994, *Foucault: A Critical Introduction*, Continuum, New York, see Chapter 3

4

Discipline and instruction

This chapter deals with Foucault's work on discipline and instruction. It ties in with the previous chapter by discussing how Foucault's understanding of power can be applied to disciplinary institutions and practices. We will focus in particular on Foucault's book *Discipline and Punish: The Birth of the Prison*, which deals with the disciplinary institutions and practices that emerged in the eighteenth and nineteenth centuries. While *Discipline and Punish* is concerned with the birth of the prison in modern Europe, it has far wider implications for the everyday lives of ordinary citizens. Notions such as micro-power, disciplinary institutions, panopticism and normative judgements—which we will discuss in this chapter—help us to understand how modern western society organises itself, and regulates people's thoughts and behaviour.

Foucault developed this material through the research methods he called archaeology and genealogy, which we discussed in Chapter 2. Basically, both methods work to uncover the discursive formations and practices of different historical periods, but genealogy has a greater focus on questions of power, and the ways in which discursive power works on bodies. Power shows itself on a subject's body because various events or happenings are 'written' on the body—they shape the way we perform, or act out, our bodily selves. An example is the way in which middle-class women, when sitting down in public, used to cross their legs at the ankle, while men would sit with their legs sprawled, or cross their legs at the knee. People didn't have to think about how they should sit—they had been instructed since childhood in the appropriate behaviour for men and women respectively, and these social rules, which had thus been 'written' on their bodies, effectively determined their bodily actions.

There is a wonderful example of how bodies have been 'trained' to act out social values in the television comedy *Frasier*. In one episode the very highly educated and culturally snobbish brothers Frasier and Nyles patronise an exclusive restaurant. They know the place well (they regularly dine there) and this is communicated in their easy, relaxed walk, the expectant expressions on their faces, the way they happily greet the manager—in fact everything about their body language tells us that they are comfortable and at home in this place. Somebody who wasn't 'at home' in exclusive restaurants would send all sorts of different signals—say, about nervousness, anxiety and contempt. Things change in the show, however, when Frasier and Nyles notice a huge, over-the-top, gaudily coloured painting of a matador and a bull hanging on the restaurant wall. Suddenly their bodies spring into action reflecting this new set of circumstances—they turn their noses up (literally), make faces, look nervously around the room. Something is wrong, and their bodies reflect this, without them being aware of what they are doing. Such events or practices often go unnoticed, or aren't consciously considered, but they play an important part in determining how we see and treat ourselves and others.

Microphysics of power

In focusing on the body Foucault traces the workings of power at a micro-level. He explicitly distinguishes his approach from studies of power that focus on the dominating role of important individuals and institutions. Foucault wants to 'cut off the king's head', as it were, so that we can recognise power not as a property of the mighty (kings, presidents, generals, accountants), but rather as a set of forces which establishes positions and ways of behaving that influence people in their everyday lives.

Foucault's notion of micro-power can be distinguished from the concept of hegemony as outlined by Italian Marxist theorist Antonio Gramsci. Gramsci argued that powerful groups don't necessarily have to impose their values on the less powerful by the use of direct force. Often, less powerful groups come to accept that the differences in levels of power and economic wealth within a society are natural and just, and so will consent to the rule of their 'betters'. When working-class people vote for conservative parties (as happened in the United Kingdom at the time of Margaret Thatcher), they are effectively agreeing that the status quo (their relative disadvantage) is the best way to organise society, and are consenting to the rule of the more privileged class. That is to say, hegemony works at the levels of people's minds, because they come to believe or think that the operations of power in society are natural and just, rather than being forced to accept social relations.

The problem with this approach, or any approach that focuses on individual belief systems or mental frameworks, is that it tends to presume, first, on the notion that there is a right and a wrong way of reasoning and, second, that subjects have the potential to make sense of the world through their capacity to reason. So, for Gramsci, hegemony was a kind of false consciousness, a mistaken view of the world, that could be corrected by showing people the truth (about how they were being dominated or exploited by Thatcher's policies, for instance). Foucault, in contrast, argues that there is no true state of existence, since our understandings of ourselves and our lives are always filtered through the ideas, discourses and institutions that constitute society.

One of these sets of discourses and institutions, of course, is the penal system. Foucault doesn't see the prison as existing only on the margins of society, put there to cater for those who have been expelled from it. Rather, he argues that we can see the prison project extending in various ways throughout society, and he charts its effect in *Discipline and Punish*. This genealogy of the prison describes the change in penal procedures in France between the mid-eighteenth and mid-nineteenth centuries. At the heart of these changes was the abandonment of torture and public executions, and the development of techniques for incarcerating criminals, working their bodies through disciplinary routines and programmes, and regulating them by practices of surveillance.

These changes coincided with the growing influence of Enlightenment philosophies based on the humanistic virtues of reason and justice, and also with the 1789 Revolution in France, which attempted to replace monarchical rule with a system of parliamentary democracy. From this perspective, it might be suspected that the change in penal procedures was tied up with the desire to find a more humane way of treating criminals than torturing and publicly executing them. But, Foucault argues, these penal changes occurred on the 'underside' of the Enlightenment project. They emerged from what were often seemingly insignificant changes in the ways in which bodies were organised and made to behave. These changes had less to do with making prisoners aware of their failings, and more to do with actively producing a kind of subject who could be identified, and treated, as a prisoner.

Rather than the new penal procedures being more rational and humane, Foucault sees them as having put in place different kinds of rationalities and logics for understanding and responding to illegal acts. These were bound up with the arrival of the more complex industrialising, urbanising and colonising societies that were beginning to replace the old feudal regimes throughout Europe from the seventeenth century. The old feudal power was being replaced by a new form of 'micro-physical' power which Foucault associates with discipline.

Discipline

We can think of discipline in two main ways which, on the face of it, seem rather different from each other. One is tied to punishment—for instance, the idea of disciplining a disobedient child. The second relates to a body of skills and knowledges: we can identify an academic discipline such as history or sociology, or we can speak of the variety of disciplines to be mastered if you want to become a rock guitarist, a ballet dancer or a professional footballer. So the first meaning understands discipline as a verb—an action we perform on other people or ourselves. The second meaning sees discipline as a noun—a set of qualities that we need to master in order to be recognised and valued within a particular field. The first meaning also views discipline as a negative force, tied up with punishment and coercive behaviour. The second values discipline as a positive force, something tied up with self-empowerment and achievement.

Foucault connects these two understandings of discipline through his concept of power-knowledge. He goes beyond the fairly conventional view that the development and acquisition of knowledge necessarily makes people more powerful, or is 'good for them'. Rather, knowledge is something that makes us its subjects, because we make sense of ourselves by referring back to various bodies of knowledge. For instance, to be a student at a school or university we must enter into different academic disciplines, and gain certificates and degrees that provide credentials which will help make us suitable for various jobs. But to be a student is also to make ourselves known to the school system, so that it can monitor our progress, pass judgements upon us, and mould our attitudes and behaviours in various ways. In these ways, discipline and knowledge 'make' us certain kinds of people.

One of discipline's concerns is with producing docile, healthy bodies that can be utilised in work and regulated in terms of time and space. In an institution like a school, for instance, a timetable regulates students' and teachers' work patterns by structuring their time so that they move from one set of skills to another throughout the day. And we can see how space can be used to regulate people by thinking of how a factory constructs different spaces, such as the different areas of an assembly line, in which people work; each person with their own tasks requiring particular skills and conferring a particular rank (floor manager, head machinist, bolt cutter). The staff can, of course, move (or be moved) from one place to another on the assembly line, depending on the needs of the institution and the abilities of the people concerned, and with each move their position in the literal and metaphorical space of the institution changes. So disciplinary power accords a person a space within an institution and a rank within a system. Such ranking enables institutions to regulate both the movement of people throughout its space and the progress they can make from one task to another. In this way, discipline individualises bodies by providing them with a location that does not give them a fixed position, but distributes them and circulates them in a network of relations, and in terms of time and space.

Foucault stresses that such discipline was not simply imposed from above. Rather, people submitted themselves to be able to operate effectively in the new social and economic conditions that were emerging in Europe during the eighteenth and nineteenth centuries. The new demands of factory production meant that people had to acquire the skills necessary to operate machinery, to manipulate implements and to endure the long days in gruelling conditions. A comparison is how an aspiring guitarist will willingly give up time to long, arduous, often repetitive and physically demanding practice in order to master the discipline. Discipline worked through such a system of punishment and gratification. People could be punished, or they could punish themselves for various indiscretions, but, at the same time, through disciplinary work it was possible to gain rewards and move up the scale—becoming a more senior factory worker (or a better guitarist).

Prison as a central disciplinary site

In the previous chapter we discussed how Foucault understands society as being divided into various fields and institutions. Disciplinary power, along with its accompanying discourses, progressively colonised these fields and the subject bodies that occupied them. Foucault emphasises that this was not a unified, coherent project or deliberate policy, but rather happened piecemeal, being evident early on in some areas and slower to emerge in others. For Foucault, the development of the prison system in the eighteenth and nineteenth centuries was a particularly rich site in which to see the emergence of disciplinary forces.

The prison emerged as a central institution in society because it was a site in which the coercive force of disciplinary power could be used in a direct and overt way. As offenders against the values of society, prisoners could legitimately be regarded as subject bodies upon which the disciplinary forces of society could be imposed. So the supposed rehabilitation of prisoners involved them being coerced, monitored, trained, made to perform routine tasks in a repetitive manner, subject to various tests and psychological studies, and repeatedly questioned about their behaviours, attitudes and values.

A great deal of effort (discursive and otherwise) was expended on how prisons could most effectively treat their inmates. Plans were drawn up for regulating the space of prisoners, isolating them from one another in cells, or giving them different tasks dependent on such factors as their time of incarceration or severity of offence. A whole array of machinery was created to work through the prisoners' bodies. Prisoners had to operate treadmills, were 'drilled' in labour gangs and on parade grounds, were subject to routine checks and physical examinations, and were required to perform menial tasks such as mopping floors.

The prison basically became a micro-society within the larger society. It had its own experts, hierarchies, ranks and network, and its own codes of conduct, protocols and procedures. For instance, it had an internal legal system which could punish prisoners and add years to their sentence, or alternatively award good behaviour with special favours and early parole. The prison also created its own fields of knowledge (such as criminology), while at the same time providing a focus for emerging fields of knowledge such as psychology.

As well as being a micro-society, the prison provided a model for the rest of society. In its dense web of disciplinary coercions, the prison developed and used procedures which, with modification, could be adopted in other fields. Foucault calls this trend of penal procedures moving into and colonising the wider society a 'carceral continuum', and he mentions factories, schools and military barracks as being particularly influenced by the disciplinary techniques devised in the prison. But we could go further and note how these coercive forces occur, in various ways, throughout the social body: sports and family life, religion, and systems of transport and communication all discipline the people in these institutions, organising their behaviour and regulating the place of bodies by the way they structure time, space and relations.

The panopticon

One of the ways of disciplining and managing bodies is surveillance, and to discuss this Foucault refers to the 'panopticon', which was designed by Jeremy Bentham in the late eighteenth century. Bentham's major project was to calculate how the greatest happiness for the greatest number of people could be achieved and, given this, it is significant that he should have been interested in prisons. It tends to confirm Foucault's view that penal reform and prison development were central to nineteenth-century thought.

Bentham's model of the panopticon was a tower placed in a central position within the prison. From this tower, the guards would be able to observe every cell and the prisoners inside them, but it was designed in such a way that the prisoners would never know whether they were being observed or not. Prisoners would assume that they could be observed at any moment and would adjust their behaviour accordingly.

In fact, the panopticon idea was not implemented in many prisons, but Foucault sees its logic as an example of the disciplinary forces at work. In previous penal regimes, prisoners had been removed from sight either in dungeons or by transportation, but the panopticon worked on an entirely different principle—that the best way of managing prisoners was to make them the potential targets of the authority's gaze at every moment of the day. And this authoritative gaze didn't reside in a particular person; rather, it was recognised as part of the system, a way of looking that could operate as a general principle of surveillance throughout the social body. This logic of the gaze, like that of discipline, was not confined to the prison, but moved throughout the various institutional spaces in society. We can see this in the way in which authorities watch over us and monitor our behaviours: school teachers use this authoritative gaze as they move about a classroom, and so do security cameras in shopping malls and night clubs. Surveillance techniques have become a fundamental part of life in modern western societies.

The gaze, though, is not something that is simply directed against us by others—it also becomes a way of looking at our own behaviours. Part of our socialisation influences us to make ourselves the subject of our own gaze, and so we are constantly monitoring our bodies, actions and feelings. There is a gender dimension to this authority of the gaze. In modern western societies, women or girls have often been positioned as desirable objects of what is called the male gaze. In other words, a fundamental part of how females are valued within such societies, and how they value themselves, is associated with how they look. In modern western societies magazines, whether they are directed to male or female readerships, will generally have photographs of females on the cover. Heterosexual male readers are disposed to see these female models as objects of their desire, while heterosexual female readers are disposed to see them as role models who, if they work upon themselves enough, they might resemble and, accordingly, become desirable to the male gaze. Indeed, adolescent girls' magazines are extensively devoted to areas such as beauty hints, slimming tips, how to look great in a bikini this summer, and also promote various aids and pieces of equipment that are designed to provide a desirable look or body image. Like discipline, the acquisition of a desirable look involves a gentle (and sometimes not so gentle) punishment that females ritualistically carry out upon their bodies, plucking out facial hairs, exercising grimly in aerobics classes, pouring hot wax upon themselves, and so on. Indeed, the notion of 'tanning' seems quite literally to suggest a form of self-punishment. The point of this regime of punishment is so that the female might attract the gaze of a desirable male and be valued accordingly.

This is not to say that males are not also subject to the gaze. Adolescent males in modern western societies build their bodies up in such a way as to effectively perform sporting disciplines. Many boys aspire to become sporting heroes, such as a Superbowl-winning quarterback or a soccer star. Accordingly, they will be inclined to devote great effort to developing a body image and set of physical capacities that might allow them to achieve this goal. This male–sport, female–beauty focus is, however, subject to change. Women are increasingly inclined to regard male bodies as the objects of their desiring gaze, a theme explored in the film *The Full Monty*. And women also adjust their image of their bodies as they engage with traditionally male activities such as sport. For example, early in her career the American tennis player Chris Evert said that she was disinclined to do weight training in case it affected her femininity. Later she took up weight training in order to make herself more competitive against her rival, Martina Navratilova. The role of the gaze has also played a significant part in the field of health. In books such as *The Birth of the Clinic* and *The History of Sexuality, Volume 1*, Foucault discussed the way in which medical and psychiatric patients have been subjected to an institutionally validated gaze that monitors their every move. Doctors and psychiatrists embody this institutional gaze as they carry out their work of evaluating their patients in terms of their bodies, behaviours and attitudes. This monitoring can take the form of 'routine questioning' of patients in terms of how they are feeling, what they are thinking about and so forth. Or it can take a more direct and intrusive form of looking over and into a patient through mechanisms such as x-rays, internal probes and gynaecological examinations. Thus biomedicine acts as the most (socially and institutionally) privileged knowledge of the body.

Other health workers, such as nurses, often stand in for doctors in performing this monitoring role. When we say people are acting out the role of the doctor's eyes and ears, we are pointing to their role as monitors and embodiers of the gaze.

On a wider social level, the gaze is a mechanism for the monitoring and control of public health. In the nineteenth century, for example, there were consistent efforts by civil authorities to 'clean up' urban spaces which had become repositories of disease and other manifestations of social unease, such as crime, unemployment, poverty and substance abuse. This involved organising surveys of the conditions of life and moral attitudes among people living in slum areas of large cities such as London, New York and Sydney. These surveys made public health into a moral as much as a social problem.

In other words, if the lower classes who resided in these areas were found to exhibit symptoms of alcohol abuse or crime, it was these factors that were perceived to threaten the public health and which then needed to be addressed and 'cleaned up'. In this way the lower classes were made subject to, and subjected themselves to, the moralising gaze of civil authorities. We see this tendency today in the way in which fields such as the popular press make their readers ever subject to 'moral threats' from within their own areas, such as paedophilia, drugs and crimes against property. Only by constantly monitoring these moral threats, it is implied, can the public health of the community be maintained.

In short, the power of the gaze, taken from the prison

project, establishes an 'economy of looks' that distributes value throughout the social body. Not only are people valued in terms of their looks; valuable activities, such as acquiring knowledge, are understood in terms of a series of visual metaphors, such as insight and vision, so that the idea of looking (or gazing) is associated with power, knowledge and value.

All these disciplinary procedures, and the panoptic gaze, emerged at an historic moment when it had become necessary to produce a pliable, healthy and sober workforce to service the factories of the Industrial Revolution. More recently, at least in western societies, the need for workers in industrial factories has declined, and there has been a growth in post-industrial, high technology fields such as computer science. With this reduced need for an industrial-style workforce, have we seen a decline in the disciplinary techniques that produced such a workforce? What we can argue is that these techniques are now not so directly apparent in fields of work, but rather they have become more evident in fields of play. The emergence of a particular culture associated with gymnasiums is an example of this trend.. Gyms employ a whole range of activities, machinery, techniques and subject positions that entail the gentle punishment and quiet coercion of disciplinary power. Gym users are monitored by professionals as they go about transforming their bodies through lifting weights, walking on treadmills, riding exercise bikes and so on. And the presence of mirrors throughout many gyms disposes users to monitor themselves, to develop a disciplinary gaze that they direct upon themselves in order to gain a sense of self-empowerment. That the techniques of discipline and 'gentle punishment' have crossed the threshold from work to play shows how pervasive they have become within modern western societies.

Descending individualism

The power of the gaze helps activate one of the fundamental principles of modern western cultures, which Foucault calls 'descending individualism'. Feudal societies operated according to the principle of ascending individualism: that is, the more powerful people were, the more individuated they could be. Peasants tended to be grouped together as an undifferentiated mob while, higher up the social ladder, individual traits were allowed to come into focus. At the highest point of the social ladder, grand displays of the monarch's power confirmed the authority and majesty of the person of the king or queen.

In modern societies, which are regulated through the authority of the gaze and associated disciplinary apparatuses, we become more individuated the further down the scale we are. So the child is monitored through school examinations, employees are monitored through progress reports, and the poor are monitored through numerous government surveys into their living conditions, moral habits and work history. An example of this descending individualism is how populist newspapers and television programmes devote coverage to suspected cases of welfare fraud among the poor, naming the perpetrators of such 'outrages' (through headlines such as 'Single mum Cindy rips off the system'), while ignoring the more costly fraudulent activities of very wealthy groups and people. Indeed, it can be argued that extremely wealthy and influential individuals have the power to avoid the scrutiny of the gaze and so protect their interests. For example, it would be virtually unthinkable that any of the many newspapers or television channels owned by the media magnate Rupert Murdoch would devote space to an investigation of their proprietor's tax minimisation schemes.

We do need to qualify this idea of descending individualism. It is evident that celebrities, who comprise one of the wealthy groups within society, tend to be strongly individuated through popular media discourse, often referred to either by first names ('Tom and Nicole', for example, for actors Tom Cruise and Nicole Kidman) or by nicknames ('Fergie' for the Duchess of York), as well as through the surveillance techniques deployed by 'paparazzi' photographers. Indeed, it might be that one of the reasons the people responded so deeply to the death in 1997 of Diana, Princess of Wales, was because they empathised with a person so thoroughly individuated and subjected to surveillance.

One effect of this descending individualism is that part of the pleasure of popular culture in contemporary western societies is associated with the desire to become part of an undifferentiated mass. There is pleasure in being part of a heaving mob on the dance floor or in the mosh pit at rock concerts, where bodies seem free of disciplinary coercions. This bodily excess recalls Foucault's point that one of the motivations for the abandoning of public executions in favour of a 'gentle' disciplinary power, with its accompanying mechanisms of descending individualism, was that the mob who gathered for the executions was an unruly, and therefore unpredictable, mass who might just turn on the executioners. Similarly, people who today are defined as part of a large group—'mass rallies' of demonstrators, 'hordes' of football supporters, or the seething 'mob' at rock concerts—are often depicted by disciplinary authorities as being a problem. And surveillance cameras are often located at such sites in order to individualise these masses, to fix a name and identity to a person in a football crowd, for example.

In short, disciplinary power and surveillance produce a complex play of visibility and invisibility. The principle of descending individualism indicates that people are made to appear as specific individuals, but the terms of this appearance are dictated by the forms of the disciplinary forces. The way in which people are made subject to various physical, academic and psychological examinations; the way in which people are required to carry identity papers; the way in which females are characteristically valued in terms of their looks: all these are examples of the disciplinary power of the gaze.

Norm and scandal

Another way in which penal disciplines have influenced the wider society has been in their focus on norms. Prisons set up ranges of procedures that establish what is considered 'normal', and evaluate the behaviours of prisoners in relation to this norm. In fact, people only become prisoners because they have been defined as having violated some social norms: as abnormal subjects, they can properly be made the subjects of a fully coercive system.

Indeed, Foucault argues that rather than really attempting to rehabilitate prisoners so that they might legitimately re-enter mainstream society, prisons are concerned with fixing prisoners in terms of their abnormal status. Certainly, penal procedures tend to confirm prisoners as having a criminal identity. They do this partly by defining 'criminals' not only in terms of the crime they have committed, but also in terms of their life more generally. We can see this process at work particularly in the case of serial killers or people who have committed major crimes such as assassination or celebrity slaying. There is considerable concern with what it is/was about a person—their background, experiences, family life and so on—that (pre)disposed 'the criminal' to commit such a crime.

Penal procedures also confirm criminal identity because prisons are like factories producing a brand of personal identity that is different from the social norm—the identity of 'the delinquent'. Because most people don't want to become delinquents, they accept the normative values that are supposed to make them 'good' citizens. Delinquency also tends to support the social inequalities which characterise most western societies. That recidivist prisoners (occupational criminals, or habitual re-offenders) tend to be from poorer economic backgrounds is, in a sense, typical of a social system in which the economically advantaged are seen as normal and good, while the economically disadvantaged can be regarded as being abnormal and bad.

Foucault suggests that the judges of normality are everywhere, throughout the social body. This process of distinguishing people on the basis of their perceived normality is an example of what Foucault calls dividing practices. Dividing practices operate throughout various social institutions such as hospitals, dividing the healthy from the sick; psychiatric clinics, dividing the sane from the mad, or the heterosexual from the homosexual; prisons, dividing the lawful from the criminal; and so forth. Dividing practices work to qualify or disqualify people as fit and proper members of the social order. We are continually being judged in terms of the normality or otherwise of our mental attributes, our physical capacities, our feelings and attitudes, and our sexual preferences. And modern western societies as a whole, along with the disciplinary institutions that comprise them, organise their practices through actively producing scandalous identities or subject roles, such as the delinquent, who serve as the 'other' against which normality can be measured. But the institutions themselves often engage in scandalous practices. It is notable, for instance, that the four disciplinary sites Foucault refers to in *Discipline and Punish*—the prison, the school, the army barracks and the workshop—all display characteristics which are closer to the terrors of the old system of spectacular punishment and torture than the new regime of gentle punishment and discipline. The scandal of sodomy and beatings features in discussions of the prison; schools (particularly boarding schools) are understood in terms of the fearful threat of beating, bullying and buggery; the scandal of bastardisation informs studies of life in army barracks; and to examine what one, albeit fictional, Foucault reader thought of the workshop, it is worth considering the impressions of Dr Robyn Penrose, Temporary Lecturer in English Literature, when she visits a modern engineering works in David Lodge's novel, *Nice Work*. Dr Penrose comments: 'You could represent the factory realistically by a set of metonymies—dirt, noise, heat and so on. But you can only grasp the meaning of the factory by metaphor. The place is like hell' (Lodge 1988: 178). Scandalous individuals and scandalous practices together make up a logic of 'the scandal' which infects every institution, and which gives an impetus to the disciplinary work of the institution in order—paradoxically—to monitor and control the threat. So institutions, and the subject roles they make available, are constantly being judged in terms of their relative normality or abnormality.

Conclusion

In this chapter we have described the theories of disciplinary power found in *Discipline and Punish*. We have shown how the 'quiet coercions' and monitoring gaze associated with disciplinary forces have become pervasive throughout the social body of modern western cultures. That these techniques derived from, and were given impetus by, the development of the prison, indicates how central and influential an institution it is in these societies. In distinguishing his approach from those models that understand power in terms of force imposed from above, Foucault shows that:

- discipline works through a series of 'quiet coercions' working at the level of people's bodies, shaping how they behave and how they 'see' the world;
- the prison developed as a prime disciplinary institution, modelling techniques that circulated throughout the social body as a whole;
- a form of surveillance based on the panopticon prison model disposed people to monitor themselves and others regarding the appropriateness or otherwise of types of behaviour and body shape.

Further reading

Butler, Judith 1993, *Bodies that Matter*, Routledge, New York
Foucault, Michel 1995, *Discipline and Punish: the Birth of the Prison*, Vintage, New York, see Part 3 'On discipline'

5

Relations of power

Power

In the previous chapter we discussed Foucault's argument that truth and knowledge, rather than being opposed to the workings of power, are in fact closely involved with it. In other words, knowledge and truth didn't just appear out of nowhere to fight for goodness, justice and progress (what we might call the 'Superman syndrome'). Foucault, in the first volume of *The History of Sexuality*, calls this the 'repressive hypothesis' of power: power dominates people, but knowledge—that is, the truth—sets people free.

This proposition permeates popular cultural texts, with the most obvious example being the dictum of the television series *X-Files* that 'the truth is out there'. *X-Files* works on the notion (or suspicion) that events around the world, and people's everyday lives, are somehow influenced or controlled by a combination of aliens and government agencies working to repress the truth about those alien visitors. What drives the show (or at least agent Mulder) is this 'quest for the truth'—it seems that all the concerns, problems, discontents, dissatisfactions, worries and neuroses of both agent Mulder (and he has those in bucket loads) and the human race will somehow be relieved or overcome once 'the truth' ('aliens did it!', 'the government is lying to you!', 'my milkman is from Mars!') is revealed.

Foucault doesn't accept this proposition. On the contrary, he argues that knowledge and truth are produced out of power struggles (between different fields, disciplines and institutions) and they are used to authorise and legitimate the workings of power. For instance, a person could be categorised as a deviant simply because the human sciences have produced such a category (say, 'the homosexual') and its characteristics and consequences ('they can't control themselves, and shouldn't teach in schools or serve in the armed forces'). Against this idea of power as being opposed to and by truth and knowledge, Foucault develops something very different—the notion of 'biopower', which can be understood as technologies that were developed at the same time as, and out of, the human sciences, and which were used for analysing, controlling, regulating and defining the human body and its behaviour.

Foucault identifies two main contexts for understanding the development of biopower. The first of these, which will be discussed in more detail in Chapter 6, was the change in the way that the state worked. Whereas prior to the seventeenth century the state was mainly seen as a means to an end—the glory of the sovereign, the welfare of the people—from the seventeenth century onward the state came to be seen as an end in itself. In other words, what mattered was the strength, wealth and power of the state. Its people were now thought of not as ends in themselves (with rights and duties), but as resources which had to be used and taken care of, in their everyday activities, to ensure the development and viability of the state. Think back to our example in Chapter 3 about the way the crew of the spaceship *Nostromo* were treated by the company in the film *Alien*: primarily as a resource to be used and discarded. This is an extreme example of this position.

Of course, in order to ensure that their populations were productive, states had to work out ways of keeping people healthy, strong, active, hard working and safe. That is, they had to watch, regulate and control their populations. Two things were needed to bring this about—a body of knowledge and an administrative apparatus. The body of knowledge came through the development of a group of disciplines (the human or social sciences) which not only took 'man'—in the sense of the sovereign and self-originating subject, rather than just another living species—as their object of study, but also any factors that affected human beings (space and architecture, for instance). These sciences differed from the natural sciences, according to Foucault, in two main ways. First, they aimed not at generalised theories (say, about the origin of life, or the nature of time), but at specificities (what was the best design for an army barracks which took into account issues such as surveillance and health?). Second, Foucault suggests that the human sciences, unlike the natural sciences, were closely tied up with operating and maintaining political power.

The need for an administrative apparatus saw the development of different 'policing' institutions—not only concerned with criminal activity, but also including areas such health and welfare—which took their theories and knowledge from the human sciences. These two developments came together, according to Foucault, at the beginning of what he calls the Classical age:

> In the middle of the seventeenth century, the systematic, empirical investigation of historical, geographic, and demographic conditions engendered the modern social sciences . . . (and) technical social science began to take form within the context of administration. (in Dreyfus & Rabinow, 1986: 134)

The second development which Foucault identified is tied up with the idea of the Enlightenment. It is difficult to define the Enlightenment, but it can perhaps be best described as both a collection of ideas and attitudes (concerning freedom, equality, justice, progress and reason) and a series of political events (such as the French Revolution and the various revolutions that followed from it) which came together in the eighteenth century in Europe. The Enlightenment sought to replace the old order of absolute sovereignty, injustice, ignorance and superstition with an order based on 'enlightened reason and rationality'.

The vampirisation of the Enlightenment

These two developments—state policing and control of populations, and the part played by the human sciences in producing technologies of regulation, on the one hand, and ideas of progress and reform, on the other—are in a sense quite different, and even antithetical, to one another. After all, while the Enlightenment ideals wanted to free people from domination and control, the knowledge and technologies associated with what Foucault calls 'biopower' wanted to do the exact opposite—to control, regulate and dominate people, to make them 'docile bodies'. The question Foucault asks is, how did the ideals, theories and discourses of freedom, revolution and Enlightenment come to be 'taken over' by the procedures and practices of biopower?

In texts such as *Discipline and Punish* and the first volume of *The History of Sexuality* Foucault produces what Michel de Certeau calls 'a Freudian story' of the 'vampirisation' of Enlightenment discourses by the apparatuses, techniques and mechanisms that characterise, and provide the impetus for, the development of 'penitential, educational and medical control at the beginning of the nineteenth century' (Certeau 1984: 45). Disciplinary procedures take over the Enlightenment project, riding on the back of the ideology of revolution: 'All the while', Certeau reminds us, 'ideology babbles on' (1984: 46). In other words, while the ideals of the Enlightenment (justice, liberty, equality, reason) were supposed to reform society (in areas such as prisons, education and health), what actually happened was that a set of disciplinary techniques, quite different from Enlightenment ideals, virtually took over the running of institutions (the army, schools, hospitals), and organised the way in which power operated in society.

Although these procedures inhabit and feed off Enlightenment ideologies, they appear to have no place of their own. Techniques suddenly spread throughout social space to the extent that they, and not Enlightenment ideals, triumphed. The question that needs to be asked is how does a set of techniques and procedures establish itself without having any official status?

Certeau looks for the answer in the Freudian narrative of the unconscious and the return of the repressed. Why do disciplinary techniques 'win out' in the end? The techniques of observation, regulation and control that culminated in what, for Foucault, is our contemporary system of power, successfully vampirised the Enlightenment project because there was something in the conditions of the time and place which encouraged their growth. If the Enlightenment got rid of the divine king and set up, in his place, the 'empty space' of democracy, then the question remains as to how the state was to function (for instance, how was a population to be organised, educated and controlled?) without direction, and without being kept under careful scrutiny? In a sense, the Enlightenment project of evacuating the place of power (because power no longer belonged to, nor could it be associated with, anyone) can also be understood as an invitation to power to conceal itself.

Kafka's story *The Castle* shows how this idea works. A man is summoned to the castle apparently because of something he has done wrong, but he can't find anybody to tell him what he's charged with. He moves through the various areas of the castle searching for answers, but nobody actually 'knows' why he's there. He has been brought into 'the system', and now can't get out. Eventually he is executed without ever knowing what his crime was. In some ways he is a forerunner of Mulder in the *X-Files*: the reason why Mulder is unable to discover the 'truth' is because nobody really knows what it is. Knowledge and information are shared across different government agencies, and there is no one person who is 'the king', who is in the centre, and able to explain everything. We tend to think of the president of the United States as being the most powerful person on earth, but as a whole series of films, from *Dr Strangelove* to the more recent *Mars Attacks* testify, the president isn't really allowed to know too much at all.

In a sense the king could always know everything because he (or she) was the one who determined (as God's representative on earth) what the truth was. But these days there is so much information floating about (on radio, television, the internet) that it becomes difficult to know what to believe—was Princess Diana killed by the British Secret Service? By Mossad? By the Devotees of the Great White Ram? We'll never know. So much 'information' has been created about the event that it will be impossible to get to 'the truth'. And, just as information and knowledge are diffused and multiplied across a culture, so is power, in the form of different systems of government and regulation. If the man in *The Castle* had been able to find a single person who was in charge he might have had a chance, but 'the system' was in charge, and if the system had identified him, then he had to be guilty.

This is one of the most important of Foucault's insights with regard to power—that it is more effective when it is hidden from view. In other words, although knowledge and technologies are being used to control and regulate individuals and populations, the official version of things is that they are 'working in our interests', 'taking care of us', looking after us and watching over us 'for our own good' ('the system is working for you'). Let's look at an example which Foucault deals with at great length in *Discipline and Punish*, and briefly sketch the change that Foucault traces in the way in which punishment was carried out up until the end of the Renaissance (a period of absolute monarchy or sovereignty), through the Classical and Modern epistemes.

In *Discipline and Punish* Foucault describes in detail both how criminals were punished and how criminal activities were understood before the coming of prison reforms. There is a particularly horrific—and minutely detailed—description, at the beginning of the book, of the torture and execution of Robert François Damiens (1714–57), a French soldier who attempted to assassinate King Louis XV, whose body was slowly and deliberately torn to pieces in front of a large crowd (Foucault 1995: 3). Today most of us would view this as cruel and barbaric—as did the penal reformers of the eighteenth century. But the punishment had its logic or rationale. Power belonged to the king, and when one of the king's subjects acted against him, the infamy of his crime had to be 'written', so to speak, on his body. Punishment, in this way, was a way of signalling to—or, actually, performing for—the citizens both the nature of the power of the king and the consequences of opposing it.

In the Classical age such spectacles were considered barbaric, and were replaced with a 'reformed system' which tried to measure exact but 'humane' punishment for crimes, and 'rehabilitate' criminals. But what gradually happened was that these ideals of reform and rehabilitation were taken over by techniques which effectively functioned in terms of providing resources for, and protecting, the state. People in gaol were no longer treated as being ends in themselves who could be reformed (through education or counselling). Instead, they became both enemies of the state and wasted resources. They had to be 'rewritten' as people so that they could make a contribution to increasing the power and wealth of the state. What this involved was the ordering and arranging of every part of their prison life, so that they became convinced that state power was everywhere and inescapable. In this way they would become 'docile bodies', automatons more or less produced by technologies of power.

One technique, discussed in the previous chapter, was the panopticon. But this isn't the appropriate place to discuss these techniques in detail, or even to evaluate whether or not they actually worked. The important point is that what looks like a straightforward move from cruel and barbaric practices (torture, dismemberment) to what were supposed to be more 'humane' practices which were meant to rescue the criminal from the life of crime that he or she had fallen into (because of poverty, or a lack of education or good examples) turned out to be something else. The hidden power at work here was introduced in the name of the ideals of reform, but actually functioned to dominate and mould people in order to make them more serviceable for the state.

It is interesting to speculate as to how this attitude of seeing people as resources or commodities tied in with the development of capitalism. There are obviously strong connections, but Foucault is unwilling to reduce the rise of biopower to being a side-effect of capitalism. On the contrary, he claims that to no small extent it was the disciplinary technologies of biopower which facilitated the development of capitalism. Foucault's argument is that biopower helped capitalism in two important ways: first, by providing a healthy, active, disciplined population as a workforce; and second, because the very detailed and function-specific arrangements of space and people that occurred in places like schools and army barracks provided the organisational models for nineteenth-century factories.

Power—general propositions

In elaborating his notion of biopower, Foucault put forward a number of general propositions about how power actually works, and can be characterised, in the post-Renaissance period.

His first major point is that power isn't a thing that is either held by, or belongs to, anybody. In the time of absolute monarchs the king or queen was able to exercise power because it belonged to them—they had received the 'gift' of power from God. But, in the Classical and Modern ages, the place of power is evacuated—power belongs to no-one. Even when monarchs continued to reign, they no longer held a position of power on the basis of their 'person'. When the English parliamentarians executed Charles I in 1649, and the French revolutionaries executed Louis XVI in 1793, they were demonstrating, among other things, that they certainly didn't believe in the divine right of kings—Charles and Louis were not God's representatives as far as they were concerned.

Neither, it was felt, did God authorise and decide who was to hold power—the state, through its various clusters of forces, did. There is a wonderful example of this change of attitude in an old film about the French Revolution. Some of the king's devoted servants are trying to help Louis XVI flee from the revolutionaries, but he is caught and taken back to Paris to be executed. One of the revolutionaries goes back to the king's room and finds his maid kneeling in front of what looks like the king, but it is just his uniform—his crown, his glittering clothes, his jewellery, his shoes—'dressed' on a clothes-horse. From now on, the 'uniforms' of power will remain in place, but they will be empty.

As far as Foucault is concerned, power now functions in terms of the relations between different fields, institutions, bureaucracies, and other groups (such as the private media and other businesses) within the state. What characterises these relations of power is that they are not set in stone. Power can flow very quickly from one point or area to another, depending on changing alliances and circumstances. In other words, power is mobile and contingent. Think of the situation which brought about the fall of the former USSR. Newspapers in the West seemed to think that the various Soviet presidents—Khruschev, Breznev, Andropov, Gorbachev—were like absolute monarchs, whereas, in fact, their decisions always depended on negotiations and alliances between influential party members, the military, scientists, bureaucrats, the presidents' families and close friends, media figures, people who ran the black markets, diplomats, the KGB and politicians. Gorbachev's attempts to reform the Soviet system depended on him being able to bring institutions such as the party, the military and the secret police with him. When the alliances between these different groups broke down, Boris Yeltsin stepped in because he could claim to be speaking for, and have the support of, 'the ordinary people'. This swung things his way—it seemed as if the momentum was with him, so many groups and individuals moved to support him. Mikhail Gorbachev went, in a very short time, from being one of the most powerful men on earth to being 'an empty suit'.

Power had moved elsewhere, and Boris Yeltsin ended up in Gorbachev's 'uniform'.

Why is power, in post-Renaissance ages, so fluid and changeable, and dependent on alliances, negotiations and circumstances? We have pointed out that the site of power—say, the 'emperor's clothes'—is now empty and potentially able to be filled by anybody. One of the reasons for this is that prior to and during the Renaissance there was, what we could call, a relative homogeneity and unity of authorised discourses. Put simply, what this means is that there were only a few people or institutions which were authorised to, or could, communicate in a public way—the monarchy, the church, the universities, artists. And most of what was written, spoken, painted or sculpted tended to support and reproduce the status quo—that is, the authority of church and monarchy. For a long time the church had a virtual monopoly over writing, and if there was a person or institution that spoke against the authorised discourses of the time, the consequences could be quite drastic.

In Chapter 2 we pointed out that, for Foucault, the Renaissance episteme saw the world as God's book. This world-view was reinforced because of the domination of writing, knowledge and culture by the church. When the church lost its power to monopolise and authorise discourses, a large number of fields, disciplines and institutions sprang up and competed with one another to authorise and produce truth and knowledge. However, because none of these groups were 'authorised by God', their claims were always being contested. No one institution, field or discourse could claim undisputed access to 'the truth', and so groups that were trying to control or influence matters of state had to negotiate and gain support for their agendas, policies or ideas.

There is an idea that, in the modern age, power comes from the people. This is based on the idea that, at least in democracies, the people elect their leaders. However, if we look at history in the twentieth century we will find that it is not a case of the people holding power, or even delegating power to individuals or groups, but a case of groups becoming powerful by 'standing in' for the people, or by claiming to speak for or represent the people. In a sense 'the people' don't really exist—politicians and other groups are continually inventing 'the people' to support and authorise their causes and claims to power. Hitler claimed to be the only truly authentic representative of 'real Germans'. In the United States during the 1950s Senator McCarthy was able to exercise great influence over American internal affairs by setting himself up as someone who spoke and acted on behalf of the people. And today, throughout the world, populists grab political office because they have set themselves up as 'standing in for' and 'sharing' the hopes, aspirations and values of the people. Of course none of this lasts very long. The people soon discover that the group who promised to look after them have ended up looking after themselves. And the party that gets elected on an anti-politician platform ends up acting like politicians.

The point Foucault would make, however, is that the people cannot 'hold' power any more than politicians or businesspeople or even, as the public demonstrations and riots in Indonesia in the late 1990s demonstrated, the military. Power moves around and through different groups, events, institutions and individuals, but nobody owns it. Of course certain people or groups have greater opportunities to influence how the forces of power are played out. Silvio Berlusconi, the former Italian prime minister, owned nine television stations, and so had considerable ability to influence what people knew or thought. Rupert Murdoch influences politicians and governments throughout the world because of his extensive media interests. Boris Yeltsin remains (1999) in power in Russia largely because of the support of business, the media and foreign governments. At the same time, there is no guarantee that having media or business interests or support will translate into, say, electoral success. In Russia the media lost influence over popular opinion because it was so clearly aligned with Yeltsin—and its claims of impartiality or to be 'telling the truth' have suffered because of this. And in Australia public opinion strongly went against the introduction of a goods and services tax precisely because the tax was supported by powerful business people and the media.

The other reason that power isn't held by and doesn't belong to the people is that, for Foucault, not only are the people, as an organic group, 'invented' by politicians and others, but people are themselves produced by, and subject to, the forces of biopower. The way people come to understand the world, the way they behave, the values and aspirations they develop and the way in which they react to events: all these things are fashioned out of the various apparatuses and technologies of biopower. So it's not as if people have independent minds and free will which might allow them to choose who will represent them, or what political system will best look after their interests, or even what their best interests are. Those kinds of things—what the French sociologist Pierre Bourdieu calls 'habitus' and 'dispositions'—are already 'the 'effects' of power or, to be more specific, the effects of biopower.

This leads to another important point that Foucault makes about power, which is that although power acts on people in a non-egalitarian way (that is, some groups are dominated and exploited and abused by the workings of power), at the same time it acts on everybody—the dominant as well as the dominated. As we pointed out in the previous paragraph, everybody is, to some extent, the product of biopower, because everybody is worked and 'written on' (in the sense outlined in the first section of Chapter 4—that the way in which we live within our bodies is already shaped) by institutions such as the family, schools, universities, bureaucracies, medical and health agencies, prisons, youth organisations, religions or the army, either directly (through being part of that institution) or indirectly (through the circulation of discourses throughout the culture). Even the most dominant of groups or individuals in a state or culture (say billionaire business people in America) are 'written' by various institutional contexts, ideas and discourses.

The media magnate Rupert Murdoch is a good example here. Murdoch's seemingly insatiable desire to expand his business interests, take over companies, control the media and influence governments looks very much like an uncontrollable drive, a kind of empire building for its own sake. What Murdoch wants, it seems, is to control things, which could be read as an indication that he is not autonomous—in control of himself—but is being 'written' by discourses of business and economic power. This obsession with the workings of business, the media and economics exists side-by-side with a barely concealed disdain for other areas of the state or society such as bureaucracies, welfare mechanisms, and the field of cultural production (particularly high culture such as ballet or opera). Everything Murdoch touches is reduced, in a sense, to a part of his strategy of empire building. Even supposedly culturally sacred areas such as baseball (in America) and soccer (in Britain) are 'alienated' by Murdoch's take-overs (buying the Los Angeles Dodgers, controlling the televising of soccer games). The very idea of Murdoch, or other business empire builders, understanding or treating sport or the arts or welfare as ends in themselves, rather than as something to be overcome or the means to extend their empires, is almost unthinkable. And this, ironically enough, from a group whose collective motto, as high capitalists, might be 'freedom of choice'.

Rupert Murdoch provides an excellent example of Foucault's contention that the process of producing 'docile' bodies and minds is not confined to state institutions and discourses watching over, regulating and controlling people's thoughts and behaviour. The basic idea of biopower is to produce self-regulating subjects. In other words, once our bodies and minds have been formed and formulated in particular ways, we then take it upon ourselves to make sure that we function in these ways, and remain good, healthy subjects. Schools, universities, psychologists, the courts, businesses and the police can only keep us under surveillance some of the time. Keeping people under surveillance all the time is a very costly exercise.

Biopower partly overcame this problem by transferring, in the nineteenth century, many regulatory functions (that had been the responsibility of the state) partly or wholly to the family and, in particular, to the mother of the family. So mothers became surrogate agents, in a sense, for schools, religions and medical agencies. In Britain in the nineteenth century, mothers were assigned the national responsibility of ensuring that the future and current resources of the state were properly developed and kept on the straight and narrow. Husbands and daughters and sons had to be healthy, disciplined and efficient workers, and mothers had much greater direct and continuous access to these 'resources' than did the institutions of the state.

But the most economical form of surveillance is, of course, self-surveillance. Once people have become docile, they continually check to make sure that they are not doing things that are unhealthy. There is an excellent example of this in the British science fiction comedy series *Red Dwarf*, where the main character, Lister, a working class 'lad', confides to the robot Kryten that he once did a 'disgraceful thing'—he 'visited a wine bar'. When Kryten enquires what is so terrible about wine bars, Lister explains that visiting a wine bar would have been the first step in becoming a class traitor. Next thing, he says, he would be 'having relationships' instead of 'going out with someone', and 'playing squash every Tuesday night with someone called Gerald'. Lister is never likely to become anything but a working-class lad with working-class values and aspirations, because he watches himself closely, night and day, for signs of 'unhealthy tendencies' (such as drinking wine, appreciating high culture or playing 'middle-class' sports such as squash).

Power and resistance

Up to this point we have given the impression that, for Foucault, there is very little escape from the forces of power, and that biopower and its technologies and apparatuses do exactly what they claim to do—regulate and control human thoughts and behaviour. However, for Foucault that is only one side of things. If we return to the opening paragraph of *Discipline and Punish*, with its description of the public torture and execution of the regicide Damiens for his attempted assassination of the king, we see an old-fashioned example of the exercising of power (a public spectacle, the 'sin' written in blood on the offender). But this still points out one important principle that Foucault insists upon—that power never achieves what it sets out, or claims, to do.

In the opening to *Discipline and Punish* we are presented with a bit of a puzzle. What do we make of these accounts of juridical violence that Foucault puts before us? As Damiens is 'written' (out of existence) by the sovereign's implements of torture, we are presented with another side of this 'horror show'—it doesn't function very well. The law comes across as an ass that can't even work out how many horses it takes to tear a body apart, and the dozens of torturers and technologies only seem to be getting in one another's way. What we are shown, in the Damiens' section, is both underkill (the body just can't be made to behave) and overkill (why do so many people with so much technology achieve so little?).

Now of course this is why, after the Renaissance episteme, the public spectacle was replaced by biopower—it promised to be more private, efficient and effective. But Foucault points out that there are at least two major problems with this claim. First, as we noted earlier in this chapter, there is no one authoritative discourse, institution or group in a state, but instead a number of competing discourses and groups which produce different versions of events. For instance, Foucault elaborates, in the first volume of *The History of Sexuality*, on the ways in which the bodies of the various categories of 'the people', including children, became scrutinised for signs and symptoms that would show their health and normality—or otherwise. From birth, the body is evaluated, measured, tested and categorised (by doctors, nurses, parents, extended family, educators, health officials, agents of religious groups) with the purpose of reading and determining its 'truth'. That truth—or those truths—can be obtained by comparing the body and its markers to the various discourses of knowledge produced by different institutions. While this did result in the scientifically authorised production of general categories of age (child, adolescent, juvenile), these different institutions and knowledges didn't go undisputed. While categories such as 'childhood' were generally understood as being stable ('everybody knows what a child is'), in reality they were subject to transformation and revision as new forms of knowledge were developed. Foucault writes, for instance:

> In the sexualization of childhood, there was formed the idea of a sex that was both present (from the evidence of anatomy) and absent (from the standpoint of physiology), present too if one considered its activity, and deficient if one referred to its reproductive finality; or again, actual in its manifestations, but hidden in its eventual effects, whose pathological seriousness would only become apparent later. (1978: 153)

This condition of the 'truth' of childhood (and doubtless the same applies to categories such as adolescence and youth) can be understood as both stable and unproblematic, on the one hand ('the truth of childhood is the sum of those knowledges that take it as their object') and, more problematically, as a site of discursive and institutional 'battles' (and therefore lacking in final authorisation, not the truth but a set of 'truths').

Foucault's point is that while we all think we know what a child or an adolescent is, in fact these categories have histories (childhood as we know it was probably 'invented' in the seventeenth century), and are always in the process of being transformed. Because children and youth are increasingly being targeted as markets in advertising texts, and because advertising largely functions in terms of the production of desirable lifestyles, activities and fashions, a connection is established between what was, to some extent, an inalienable part of society and culture (for instance, the decommoditised and desexualised child) and the 'irrepressible drive' of capitalism. This means that popular culture and youth/child culture have become saturated with a new set of categories and subjectivities (based on the newly and overtly sexualised child, for instance) which run straight into more traditional and unalienable (and usually official) categories and discourses about childhood and youth. The result is a cultural crisis, played out in the media, government, bureaucracies and the public sphere, about the 'threat' to children and childhood. Foucault's point, however, is that these crises are always with us, because these categories and discourses aren't natural—they are part of the 'effects of power'. And one of the reasons that people are able to resist the forces of power is precisely because people recognise this. Without any final authority to 'make people believe' (say, a belief that God has authorised these discourses or categories), we are in a sense partly free to shop around for what we will believe or accept.

There is a second reason why power doesn't live up to its claims to completely dominate our thinking, behaviour and lives. Foucault points out that power should never be thought of in purely negative terms—that it is, first and foremost, productive. Biopower and its technologies, institutions and discourses produces an almost infinite variety of categories and sub-categories of people and behaviour which compete with one another to regulate and control populations. But of course, as soon as you produce categories of what is normal, healthy and good, you produce other categories—the pervert, the deviant, the trouble-maker, the problem child, the homosexual, the hysteric, the kleptomaniac, the pyromaniac, the psychotic. In some ways, forms of social-scientific knowledge and research make these people up—bring into being the categories into which they fit, and hence produce their subjectivities—as they go along.

Perhaps the best example of how power produces something other than 'docile bodies' is the prison system. Foucault points out that while the technologies of power used in prisons are supposed to produce 'compliant' bodies and behaviour, in reality the opposite happens. Prisons, in fact, function as 'criminal factories'. Prisoners become convinced that they are all the things (deviant, lazy, evil, useless, human rubbish) that the system says they are. So prisoners are brought together where they can exchange ideas, experiences, techniques, contacts, strategies—in other words, where they can learn to be effective and efficient criminals. This is reinforced because the prison system treats them like criminals. And what we suggested about people's self-surveillance probably applies to an even greater extent to those outside the categories of normal and healthy. In this respect, power is successful in 'writing' people, but the effects are not what was intended.

Conclusion

In this chapter we have introduced one of the most important areas of Foucault's work—his ideas on power. We made the point that Foucault doesn't think of power as a thing to be owned or held by somebody, but as a ubiquitous, and ever-changing flow. The way in which this flow moves around depends very much on how different groups, institutions and discourses negotiate, relate to and compete with one another.

Foucault argues that, after the Renaissance, the notion of power being held by or identified with a single person or group such as the king/queen or church (and authorised by God) is replaced by what he calls biopower. Biopower developed with the coming of the social or human sciences, which took the human body and behaviour as its object of knowledge. This knowledge gave rise to institutions and administrative techniques for measuring, regulating and controlling people and behaviour in order to ensure that states got the most out of their human resources.

Foucault does not suggest, however, that biopower has completely regulated bodies and behaviour. Because there are so many competing ideas, institutions and discourses, no single authorised truth ever emerges to dominate a society. And, in a sense, biopower is never able to completely control things because it always produces resistance.

We can sum up the main points of this chapter as follows:

- The change in the idea of the seat of power—where power is located—from the divine rule of kings to the empty place of democracy, where power is 'owned' by no-one;
- The change in the exercise of power, from brutal and public force to hidden coercions;
- The central role of 'biopower' in controlling the bodies and the minds of subjects—but, in the process, the rules by which some people are produced as normal or healthy, and others are excluded, ensures that opposition and resistance are built in effects.

Further reading

Deleuze, Gilles 1988, *Foucault*, trans. Sean Hand, Athlone Press, London, see 'Strategies or the non-stratified: the thought of the outside'

Foucault, Michel 1978, *The History of Sexuality: Vol. 1, an Introduction*, Penguin, Harmondsworth, see Part 1

McNay, Lois 1992, *Foucault and Feminism: Power, Gender and the Self*, Northeastern University Press, Boston, see Chapter 1

6

Governmentality
and liberalism

The idea of being governed and the mechanisms of that
governance have always been a concern for people, even those
who don't take a great interest in politics. Everyone complains
that they are paying too much in taxes; corporations and
businesses want little government intervention so that they
can get on with creating wealth; newspapers are full of stories
of government bureaucracies either 'interfering' in the lives
of ordinary people ('social workers are stealing children from
their parents'), or not providing enough services to meet the
demands of the population ('we need more hospitals, schools,
doughnut shops, universities'). At the level of the state, the
balance between providing incentives for people through low
taxation has to be balanced against the need for the state to
provide basic services in areas such as health, aged care,
education, transport and unemployment. At the level of
family life, on the other hand, similar questions about how—
and how much—parents should govern or direct their
children's activities tends to be an issue of ongoing public
concern. Within every aspect of our social life, the issue of
government assumes great significance.

Foucault's contribution to theories of the art of governing
has been to draw out the links between the levels of state and
global politics, on the one hand, and the level of individuals
and their conduct in every range of life, on the other. Taken

together, this constitutes what he calls 'governmentality'. For Foucault, governmentality is as least as much a matter of 'body politics'—the ways of conducting ourselves, the relationship we have with our own bodies and the other bodies that constitute society—as it is a matter of conventional politics (political parties, elections).

While the issue of governmentality is given only limited attention in Foucault's work—it emerges most clearly in a series of essays and lectures given in the mid-1970s, around the time he was working on *Discipline and Punish* and the first volume of *The History of Sexuality*—the concept can be used to help us make sense of Foucault's work as a whole. Governmentality ties in with Foucault's more general concern with the ways in which power and its practices are linked to the processes of what he calls 'subject formation', and how an understanding of these processes can help an individual to gain a certain amount of freedom and personal autonomy. That is to say, because governmentality is as much about what we do to ourselves as what is done to us, this opens up the possibility that we might intervene in this process of self-formation. Foucault's aim is to explore the ideas and practices of governmentality, and the possibilities we have of understanding and negotiating it.

The social contract model

For Foucault, theories of governmentality can be divided into two distinct types. First there is the 'social contract' model. This position argues that states and systems of government came into existence when individuals 'agreed' to give up certain freedoms in order to benefit from banding together. In other words, people 'contracted in' to statehood and being governed—a kind of legal contract that is the basis of government. This is similar to the way in which a worker and a company might enter into an employment contract, agreeing conditions such as pay, working hours, duties and so forth. Unlike the situation of an employment contract, however, there never was a time when groups or individuals more or less calculated the advantages and disadvantages of being governed, and decided, after some soul-searching, to sign up. Theorists have to set up a make-believe time, a political fantasy, when the rule of sovereign law was 'agreed' to. The English philosopher Thomas Hobbes, one of the more important contract theorists, gets around this problem by arguing that people agree to contract in because they have no choice (that is, the choice is to agree to be governed, or refuse to agree, but you will be governed anyway, whether you like it or not).

Social contract theory is an idealised version of government which can never really overcome the absence of any initial act of consent—which is what it is based on. It tries to overcome this problem either by following the unsatisfactory Hobbesian line (it is hard to accept the notion that 'I agree to contract in freely because I have a gun at my head' can be taken as a form of consent), or by suggesting that the law (understood as the principles of liberty, equality and fraternity, for instance) existed before society was formed. This suggests that the law came into existence more or less by itself, and carried humanity and society along with it. An excellent example of this kind of story, taken from popular culture, is to be found in Stanley Kubrick's film *2001: A Space Odyssey*, where civilisation occurs because aliens visit the planet at some distant time and jump-start everything. Yet so influential has this vision of originary law been that it can be discerned as a foundational principle within a number of very different social fields—the role of 'divine law' in explaining religious accounts of the human beings' place in the world, for example, or the dependence of scientists on the 'laws of nature' for accounting for the development of the universe.

For Foucault, this idea of 'juridical sovereignty' ignores the fact that the law is something that is produced by, rather than being the originator of, the processes of history. In other words, the law is not something that is eternal and god-given. Laws are made by people, and then unmade again, depending on circumstance. Perhaps one of the best examples of this is the doctrine of *terra nullius*, which the British used to justify their 'settlement' of Australia from 1788. *Terra nullius* was the doctrine that the land belonged to no-one, meaning that the indigenous peoples of Australia were not recognised as having any claim over, or occupation of, the land. The 'Mabo' and 'Wik' decisions reached in the High Court of Australia, in 1992 and 1996 respectively, largely contradict *terra nullius* by recognising that indigenous peoples of Australia have some, albeit limited, claims to native title over the land. These decisions have changed the way in which we now understand the rights of the indigenous inhabitants of Australia with regard to British 'settlers' and British law. Previously, the law suggested that indigenous peoples had no rights; now it is accepted that they do have claims on the land. Indeed, much of the political landscape in Australia in the 1990s has been devoted to debating the appropriate limits of the claims of various parties—indigenous peoples, miners, pastoralists—to land tenure.

It can be argued that the law, rather than being the originator of the rule of justice and reason, works to cover up the acts of violence so often a part of the establishment of communities or nations. The doctrine of *terra nullius* and the crucial role it played in excluding Aboriginal peoples from the rights and privileges enjoyed by the British is, as we have seen, a good case in point. The land which the British 'settled' (Aboriginal peoples regarded it as an invasion) was ruled to be empty, or inhabited by no-one. What this meant was that the community of Australia was set up through the 'contracting in' of certain groups (the army, free settlers) but, at the same time, that community excluded other groups (Aboriginal peoples, convicts) who were denied the rights and privileges of citizenship.

These practices of 'contracting in' certain groups and excluding others have been central to the development of virtually every social order. Who legitimately belongs to a community can only be judged on the basis of knowing who is excluded. These patterns of inclusion and exclusion are subject to shifts over time. In the Australian colonies, for example, convicts moved from an excluded status to being contracted in as legitimate members of community through being assigned work for government and private interests. That convicts could attain an influential position in such a society meant that, from the perspective of other societies such as Britain, the Australian colonies themselves were tainted with a 'convict stain', and as such were excluded from the 'proper' order of societies.

The social warfare model

There is an alternative position to 'social contract' theory, based on the idea of continuous 'social warfare'. In this version, a group or groups seize power, establish themselves as dominant in a society, and set up the state in terms of their own ideas, values and self-interest. While governing is supposedly based on laws and principles that protect truth, equality and justice, in reality these are all fabrications, put in place in order to justify and maintain the dominant group's power and control. Of course this social warfare is ongoing, so one group can be overthrown by another, which then sets about rewriting history, the law, rights and values in order to keep themselves in power. The best-known version of this warfare scenario is to be found in Marxism, which makes use of notions such as ideology and 'false consciousness' to explain how domination is maintained by groups without their having to use overt force or violence.

For Marxism, history is characterised by class struggles, with the capitalist classes sometimes making use of overt forms of violence (carried out, for instance, by the military or the police) but, more often than not, using covert means to maintain their domination. The concept of hegemony, developed by the Italian theorist Antonio Gramsci (who lived under Mussolini's Fascist government), explains how states and state institutions work to win popular consent for their authority through a variety of processes which disguise their position of dominance. From this perspective, laws, institutions, and the ideals and processes of governing constitute an 'empty' performance which is meant to draw attention away from their 'real work', which is to establish the rule of one group of society (in Gramsci's Italy this was the Fascists and the wealthier classes) at the expense of others (the workers, the communists).

While Foucault agrees that governments exploit and repress people while pretending to be just and fair, he doesn't think that societies and governments are always characterised by warfare directed by one group against another. Foucault suggests that, within societies, power circulates and people are dominated and repressed, but it's more complex than simply identifying who are the oppressors, and who are the oppressed. He asks us to think beyond the explanation of perpetual social warfare, suggesting that, say, conflicts and differences between different classes do not necessarily follow a straightforward narrative (for example, 'the middle classes attack and subjugate the working class'). We pointed out in our previous chapter that, for Foucault, power in modern societies is not simply something that is gained, held, and used by individuals or groups (the way in which the emperors of Rome or the pharaohs of Egypt had complete power, which was identified with their person). Rather, he thinks of power as a complex flow—a set of relations between different groups, which changes with circumstances and time.

Take the hypothetical example of a contemporary Indonesian woman, who is also a lawyer and a Muslim, trying to work out what her 'real' political attachments are. As a Muslim she might be expected to support the local Islamic party, which was promising to help the underprivileged classes, and clean up corruption. But she is worried that an Islamic government might become fundamentalist, and introduce laws restricting the role of women in society—which would threaten her career. She could support the ruling party, which is backed by the military, the wealthy classes, and some middle-class professionals; after all, her father, a retired general, is a member of the party executive. But she dislikes the government's disregard of human rights, and identifies with reformist groups, mainly comprising students, intellectuals or professionals like herself. But she knows that if the reformists came to power, her family, closely tied to the ruling party, would lose out—her father might even go to jail. What, exactly, are her 'political attachments'? This hypothetical Indonesian is, simultaneously, a woman, a Muslim, a lawyer, a daughter, and somebody with a social conscience. In other words, her identity is split across all the major political groups.

For Foucault the idea of a straightforward social identity (based on, say, class) is difficult to accept. He makes the point that an individual's understanding of their own identity changes, depending on the circumstances. Different factors—such as gender, race, age, ethnicity and religion—may be important one day, and irrelevant the next; and we all have many (potential) identities, and belong to a variety of different groups.

Social stories

Foucault sees these two versions of society and power—social contract and perpetual warfare—not as the truth about society, but as stories produced by different historical circumstances. For instance, Foucault points to a number of specific historical contexts (sixteenth-century France and their religious wars; internal English conflicts between religious groups, the monarchy and parliament, Saxons and Normans, and aristocracy and peasantry), all of which, at different times, have been put forward as definitive explanations of all subsequent historical events. But these historical explanations of the present always give way to newer 'discoveries' of the 'real' origins of what we are and where we came from. Things are more complex than the explanation 'we are what we are today because the Normans defeated the Saxons at the Battle of Hastings in 1066'. Foucault points out that 'two types of decipherment of history will develop in the nineteenth century: one will be linked to class struggle, the other to biological confrontation' (1997: 64); and, in the twentieth century, these decipherments have helped to produce both communist and Fascist pro-grammes and ideologies. The class struggle version of history helped give rise to communist movements in places like Russia and China, while the biological confrontation version of history helped produce a kind of 'social Darwinism', sug-gesting that stronger races would prevail over weaker races, which shaped the ideologies of Fascist Italy and Nazi Ger-many. Here we see how the different stories emerging from particular historical circumstances can be taken up by interest groups as part of their political programme.

Technologies of governmentality

If Foucault is unwilling to accept either the social contract or warfare models as explanations of the history of, and changes to, governing, what does he propose in their place? He points to a number of important developments that can help us trace the emergence, and make sense, of governmentality. First, we have the institutionalising of different aspects of government. For example, whereas pastoral care (looking after the sick, the needy, and the morality of the people) was once the respon-sibility of the church, educators and physicians, gradually it came to be seen as something that the government should look after. Second, this change to the idea of what constituted government and governmental responsibility cannot be explained in terms of one group (say, bureaucrats, or the middle class) making a disguised grab for power. Rather, what happens is the emergence of a rationality ('the reason of state') which is not concerned with questions of how power can be maintained (for instance, 'how can merchants or bankers keep power?') but, instead, sets itself up as having answers to questions of government, and the well-being and prosperity of the state. So there is a movement from focusing on who has power and influence, to a rationality based on how power can be exercised most efficiently.

For Foucault this change in thinking produced two dis-tinctive types of knowledge: a diplomatic/military aspect which concerns itself with external political security; and 'policy', which is understood as a set of technologies and institutions responsible for internal security, stability and prosperity. To this pair, Foucault adds a third, decisive element—economics.

This combination of forces and technologies was, according to Foucault, extremely productive. If the state's population came to be understood, first and foremost, as a resource, then the proper role of the state was population management. This required the production of knowledges that would allow the state to scientifically analyse that population, which was followed by the introduction of policies that both regulated behaviour (for the good of the individual, which meant, at the same time, for the good of the state), and kept the population happy and healthy—and therefore productive.

Foucault calls this development 'biopolitics', and this concept was discussed in detail in Chapter 5. One of the most important points about this change, for Foucault, is that while it constituted an example of unparalleled state intervention in the lives of its citizens (through the analysis and regulation of all forms of behaviour), at the same time the state was forced to come to terms with the fact that violent and repressive government, and constant state intervention in people's lives, are not the best way to stimulate wealth and provide prosperity. People were more co-operative, and worked more productively, it seemed, when confronted with the carrot, rather than the stick.

Why was this the case? Foucault suggests that the state wanted to maintain its role of intervening in and regulating people's affairs. Otherwise, the argument went, how could the state ensure that people weren't leading unhealthy, lazy and unproductive lives? But, at the same time, it was thought that 'the free enterprise of individuals' (1997: 73) was the best principle for producing greater wealth and prosperity. This problem was dealt with, according to Foucault, through the development in Britain of a particular kind of relationship between the state, the people and the 'attitude' of liberalism.

The liberal attitude

Foucault argues that liberalism is actually a response to the strongly interventionist policies developed in the German states in the eighteenth century. Liberalism ushered in a significant change of direction for governmentality because it broke with the 'reason of state' which had emphasised interventionist policies aimed at ensuring the security and prosperity of the state. For liberalism, the state was a necessary evil—which might not even be necessary. Liberalism took advantage of the growing importance of economics to the state, and of the state's inclination to draw back from intervening, in order to ensure the free enterprise of individuals. Out of this process there develops a notion of 'civil society' as something more or less opposed to, critical of, and a check upon, government intervention in the lives of its citizens.

One of the great ironies was that when the first liberals came to power in Britain in the early nineteenth century, this was accompanied by increased government legislation (Poor Laws, Reform Bills, Education Acts), not less. All the same, liberalism is, in a sense, 'the government you're having when you're not having a government'. Responsibilities for various parts of the population and their well-being were moved from a centralised state to other private or state-funded institutions (schools, hospitals, the military, prisons, charities). At the same time, the particular practices and technologies of governing in various dispersed sites and institutions—the ways in which parents governed the welfare of their children within the family, the way in which the architecture and work arrangements of the factory governed the production of workers, for example—fed back into centralised state operations in such a way as to provide for a governmental logic which was both generalised and localised. This logic was generalised in the sense that it helped to cement the processes of regulating individual conduct throughout the social body as a whole. It was localised in that it was concerned to deploy a range of techniques and apparatuses (from a parent's monitoring of children's sexual conduct in the home, to the development of physical training procedures in schools) that impacted upon the conduct of each individual—body and soul—within the society.

It is important to understand that for Foucault the development of these two spheres—the interventionist, regulatory state and the civil society—are not separate. The 'reason of state' which promoted the existence, security and prosperity of the state as its end, produced the need for a civil society which would both criticise the effectiveness and necessity of the development of state policies of intervention and regulation and, in certain instances, replace it. Questions of what constitutes moral or ethical behaviour, for instance, were largely removed from the control of government and became matters of 'public concern'. Think of the way in which, in western society, debates about what is morally acceptable (euthanasia, homosexuality, promiscuity, abortion) are not so much driven by government policy, but by pressure groups (such as the various Moral Majority groups in the United States).

How does liberalism show itself today? As Foucault suggests, in a variety of forms, without any great consistency or predictability. For instance, Foucault makes reference, at different times, to the Chicago School of American Neo-Liberalism, whose economic policies (promoted most noticeably by Milton Friedman) influenced a number of politicians and government leaders in the West—Ronald Reagan (1980s) in the United States; Margaret Thatcher (1980s) and Tony Blair (late 1990s) in the United Kingdom; Bob Hawke (1980s), Paul Keating (to mid-1990s) and John Howard (late 1990s) in Australia; Robert Muldoon (late 1970s to mid-1980s) and David Lange (late 1980s) in New Zealand—to withdraw government from society to some extent, while giving greater rein to the free market and to individualism. Free-market economics is not the same as liberalism—but it is one of the paths that liberalism has taken during this century.

Economics, for Foucault, is a crucial point in this rethinking of governmentality and the move to a free market society. How, then, is his position different from Marxists, who argue that capitalism and capitalists effectively run governments?

Doesn't this contradict Foucault's rejection of the 'warfare' version of government? In fact, what Foucault does is argue that liberalism appeals to principles connected to the sovereignty of the law (liberty, equality and fraternity) and to the market ('free enterprise is more productive') in order to stop the encroachment of the state and governmentality, and to guarantee the relative autonomy of civil society.

How does this happen? Liberalism uses the market—and in particular the notion of the market as a space and a set of practices with a 'natural' logic and set of laws of its own—as the means of limiting or shutting out government intervention. And it uses the law in much the same way. Rather than seeking protection from the excesses of government in universal laws, liberalism attempts to make use of the law to regulate government out of society. In the United States in the 1980s, for instance, various States passed bills which were aimed at restricting government expenditure, and thus forcing them out of certain activities (welfare, health). And President Reagan was instrumental in deregulating the American air transport industry, arguing that it needed to have government off its back to become more productive.

We might explain Foucault's interest in the liberal attitude of governmentality, as an alternative to the 'social contract' and 'perpetual warfare' models, in more detail through reference to the long-running dispute, in American politics, between President Clinton and the Republican Party-dominated Congress during the 1990s. While the 'social contract' approach to governmentality is inadequate because it cannot adequately account for the distribution of interests within this dispute, the 'perpetual warfare' model is similarly unable to account for the shifting alliances between various players. The 'liberal attitude' is more apparent as a principle around which the claims of competing interests might be articulated. For example, both the president and Newt Gingrich's Republicans appealed to liberal principles in arguing for their respective policies and approaches to government.

Of course what they meant by 'liberal' differed considerably. For the president, it meant the extension of social, political and economic opportunities, by way of government legislation, to groups that had traditionally been marginalised or disadvantaged—especially the poor, women and Afro-Americans. For Newt Gingrich, it meant a kind of Darwinian competition, with the government legislating government out of people's lives and affairs. And this dispute over which liberal path to take was in no way reducible to simple party politics. On occasions, Democrats opposed the president's policies (because they thought they would be unpopular, or because they had been influenced by powerful lobby groups such as the National Rifle Association), while Republicans sometimes supported him if they felt that particular policies or initiatives were popular with the public, or suited their constituencies. This dispute over who was 'really' liberal was played out, in the best traditions of liberalism, across central government and various dispersed institutional sites, taking in the whole of American civic society.

Perhaps the best example of what we are talking about came in the 1996 United States presidential election, when the Republicans sought to label the president, pejoratively, as a 'liberal'. Clinton responded when thus tagged by Senator Bob Dole in one of the debates, 'That dog won't bite'. This is an interesting example of the unstable flow of power as expressed in naming: on the one hand, the United States prides itself on a liberal democratic tradition; on the other hand, 'liberal' can be used to signify weakness when deployed in particular contexts. This point demonstrates the Foucaultian insight that names like 'liberal' don't matter so much in themselves; rather, their meaning comes from the ways in which they are articulated and deployed by various interests within the flow of power relations. 'Liberal' is 'good' within a network of power that dissolves the exercise of government from the central state to private individuals and institutions such as families and financial companies. 'Liberal' is 'bad' when it signifies a central state perceived to be weak in particular areas where it is still held to represent the strength of the social body as a whole, such as law and order or defence.

Conclusion

This chapter has provided an introduction to two areas that are of crucial significance to Foucault's theories—governmentality and liberalism. These are important because:

- Foucault's theorising of governmentality provides the context for many other concepts—discourse, biopolitics and biopower, discipline and punishment, regulation, the production of subjectivities—that are important to his work;
- What Foucault does, in his work on governmentality, is to trace the move in Western Europe from various forms of sovereignty to what he has described as the development of technologies of governmentality;
- In doing this he puts forward a version of governmentality which is quite different from the accounts provided by Marxism and social contract theory—a version which places considerable emphasis on the 'attitude' of liberalism;

Foucault's notion of liberalism as something which emerges out of the relationship between governmental, legal and economic contexts is important for two reasons:

1 It deals with the change in Western Europe from a particular notion of governmentality as a 'reason of state' (and an 'art of governing') that puts itself forward as having a monopoly over state security and prosperity and the regulation of populations, to an awareness of the need to involve civic society in these areas of activity.
2 The description and analysis of this process of change provides a good example of Foucault's argument that power is not possessed by a group or individual, but passes through points and stages during which it is transformed and rerouted.

In other words, rather than suggesting that power completely dominates people and societies, Foucault shows, through the example of the rise of the 'attitude' of liberalism, how power always creates its own 'other', its own opposition.

Further reading

Burchell, Graham et al. (eds) 1991, *The Foucault Effect: Studies in Governmentality*, University of Chicago Press, Chicago, see Chapter 4

McNay, Lois 1994, *Foucault: A Critical Introduction*, Continuum, New York, see Chapter 3

Ransom, John 1997, *Foucault's Discipline: The Politics of Subjectivity*, Duke University Press, Durham and London, see Chapter 3

7

History and geopolitics

Foucault studied many different historical eras, from ancient Greek and Roman cultures to European societies from the sixteenth to the twentieth centuries. Yet, while a conventional image of an historian is of someone who feels 'at home' in the historical era they are investigating and recreating, Foucault's historical studies were intended to directly influence the lives of present-day readers. In this sense they can be called histories of the present. As he comments: 'I am fascinated by history and the relationship between personal experience and those events of which we are a part. I think that is the nucleus of my theoretical desires' (1998: 124).

In Chapter 2, we made the point that for Foucault, different historical periods have radically different ways of ordering experience and making sense of it. This means that a reader in the early twenty-first century cannot have access to the mind-set and style of sense-making of a person living in a different historical era. Foucault's archaeologies are not directed at either capturing the conscious thoughts and feelings of historical actors (as Hollywood has attempted to do with films about Antony and Cleopatra, Shakespeare, Queen Victoria or Rasputin), or recreating the 'truth' or essence of an historical period (*Rob Roy, Braveheart, Robin Hood: Men in Tights*). These historical periods and actors are, in a sense, inventions of our own time; we progressively reconstruct the past in order to serve the interests of the present. In this sense, the nineteenth century did not occur between 1801 and 1900, but rather is an ongoing invention that has been subject to revisions and reconstructions through each subsequent era. So rather than thinking of history as a single, fixed entity, complete unto itself, Foucault would encourage us to think of multiple, overlapping and contesting histories.

The second term with which we are concerned in this chapter is geopolitics, which refers to the way in which political events and power struggles are shaped by geographical contexts and relations between different areas of the world. Although Foucault did not devote much of his work directly to geopolitical issues, we can draw from his studies a number of insights and concepts that can help to make sense of geopolitical issues shaping the world today. This chapter, then, considers how Foucault's approach differs from that of conventional historiography (the writing of history) and how this approach has important implications for understanding geopolitical relations.

Archaeology and genealogy

Foucault's approach to the study of history was archaeological and genealogical. The archaeological side involved isolating various orders of discourse which laid down the conditions for articulating thoughts and ideas, propositions and statements through which people made sense of their historical time. The genealogical side had more to do with non-discursive mechanisms of power which shaped the way people saw the world and acted within it. So, the various discourses that make up a school curriculum (mathematical, scientific, literary) express the archaeological approach. But the organisation of the space of the school, the way in which classrooms are designed in such a way that the teacher is empowered to move about and monitor each student's behaviour, has more to do with the genealogical side. We will discuss later how both the archaeological and genealogical approaches help us to make sense of geopolitical relations. At this stage, it is worth considering how Foucault's approach differs from other ways of making sense of history.

History writing in its modern form can be dated from the early nineteenth century. Not coincidentally, this period also experienced the dramatic increase in European colonisation. This is one of the principal criticisms Foucault has of the traditional method of writing history. Foucault sees it as playing an instrumental role in the colonising process itself and is therefore unable to provide a perspective that offers a useful critique of this colonisation. Partly, for Foucault, this is because conventional history writing regards history in terms of a single and steady progress unfolding over time. This progressive view of history (sometimes called a teleological view) tends to see the world gradually evolving into some ideal state, or utopian society. From this perspective, rather than being considered as an act of violent aggression by the colonising force, colonialism is regarded as an aspect of the evolutionary development of history into higher forms of society.

The first leading philosopher of history in the modern age, Hegel, writing in the early nineteenth century, developed a theory of dialectics. This conceived of history in terms of the clash of opposite forces (thesis and antithesis) which would be resolved by the development of a synthesis between these opposing forces, and a higher state of human development. While Hegel's dialectic theory was based on a spiritual plane, related to human consciousness, Karl Marx applied this dialectic theory to the material conditions of society—the distribution of economic resources. According to Marx's dialectic materialism, the clash over material economic resources between the bourgeoisie (owners of the means of production) and the proletariat (factory workers) would be resolved through revolution. This 'dialectic' struggle would lead to a new synthesis, a communist utopia, in which the fruits of labour would be distributed to all according to their needs. It is ironic that the collapse of communist states in eastern Europe in the late 1980s prompted the American writer

Francis Fukuyama to talk of a new synthesis represented by the triumph of western-style democracies. The American president George Bush took up this idea when he spoke of a 'new world order' in the lead-up to the Gulf War in 1991. Foucault identifies a number of problems with this dialectic view of history. First, it tends to justify European colonial practice as involving the clash of an advanced civilised West with a backward and barbaric rest of the world (both Hegel and Marx were supporters of colonial practice). Second, it tends to conceive of the forces of history largely in terms of the great ideological belief systems that emerged during and after the Enlightenment: liberalism, capitalism, socialism, communism and so forth. This kind of approach to history is sometimes called the history of ideas. As we discussed earlier, Foucault is interested in how disciplinary and other forces and power relations 'vampirised' these Enlightenment discourses and ideologies. So, for example, while the ideology of liberalism preaches the values of individual freedom of expression and belief, disciplinary power was working through sites such as schools and workshops to quietly coerce people into forms of behaviour and attitudes of mind amenable to the interests of these disciplinary institutions and the larger societies they helped constitute.

A third problem Foucault has with the dialectic and similar models of history is that they understand history according to a grand or totalising vision. That is, they suggest that we can fit the various events that take place over time into a pattern, according to certain laws of historical development. Against this synthetic view of history (the idea that different events can be synthesised to form a coherent whole), Foucault conceives of history in terms of plurality—a multiple number of events that are as often and as much in conflict with one another as they can be held together.

This is the key to Foucault's genealogical approach, which tries to trace out the multiple beginnings, sudden lurches forwards, pauses and gaps which, for him, comprise historical events. So history is conceived of in terms of discontinuity and disjuncture, rather than continuity and conjuncture. That is, rather than seeing historical time unfolding in an orderly, continuous, linear manner in which various historical events can be conjoined or fitted together to form regular patterns, we need to recognise history in terms of an ongoing chaotic struggle between different forces, and according to different levels—or patterns—of time.

Speaking positions of history

Not only is there a disjuncture and discontinuity between different historical events, there is also a disjuncture and discontinuity between historians and the historical events they seek to describe. The historian and history 'speak' from different places. The historian speaks from a credentialised position within a public institution such as a museum, archive or university. The historian may engage in field-work and archival search, but it is the protocols and procedures of the institution which will shape how the history will be written, and how the different historical events will be fitted together to form a coherent vision.

While the historian speaks from a single, officially sanctioned and institutionalised place, history 'speaks' from everywhere and nowhere. Historical events resonate not merely through the archives that have been collected, but also through its gaps—the historical material that has been lost or has not been collected. For example, the oral histories of indigenous peoples, or the folk tales of European peasants find no place within the written historical records, but they continue to 'haunt' this record through their silences, opening up gaps within the historiographic enterprise. An excellent example of this is the way in which historians—and academics and school teachers—have presented the 'discovery' of America by Colombus, and the subsequent colonising of Central and South America, in a very positive light.

In western culture Colombus has been celebrated as a great hero (despite the fact that he never actually made it to America, and thought he had landed in India), but to mark the five hundredth anniversary of his arrival in the Americas, indigenous peoples in Central and South America held a mock trial of Columbus, found him guilty of causing genocide, and sentenced him to death (in absentia—and belatedly). The point they made was that Colombus indirectly brought about the death of millions of people. There have been suggestions made that within twenty years of Spanish colonisation the indigenous population of South America had been reduced from twenty to two million people—which of course is much worse than anything the Nazis did. And yet Colombus and the Spanish have been celebrated as heroes in historical texts, mainly because nobody really cared about, or considered, how the indigenous population saw things.

This 'revision' of historical events is being popularised in contemporary culture. For example, historians tended to write about the creation of the United Kingdom (England, Scotland, Wales and Northern Ireland) as if it were a good thing, and an inevitable occurrence, but movies such as *Braveheart* and *Rob Roy* (and the Hong Kong film *Once Upon a Time in China*) show a different side of things—they depict the English as ruthless, violent invaders terrorising and enslaving innocent people. Again, this side of things has more or less been suppressed by western historians, academics and teachers because nobody took the Scottish or Welsh or Irish (or Chinese) perspective into account.

The founding subject

In challenging the authority of the historian, Foucault draws attention to another problem with much conventional historiography—that is, it begins with the notion of the unified subject. This view of history is that historical events occurred as a consequence of the various motivations of different historical actors. Accordingly, it is the duty of historiography to work through these motivations and recreate the thought patterns and feelings of the significant historical figures. This approach belongs to the 'great men of history' school which focuses on the lives of leading monarchs, politicians, explorers and warriors such as Henry VIII, Richard Nixon, Christopher Columbus and Adolf Hitler.

For Foucault, this approach misses the point that, rather than people being the originators of their own actions and makers of their own meanings, their actions and meanings are shaped by the discursive and non-discursive forces which flow through the positions these figures occupy. What discourses was Hitler drawing on, or speaking through in order to be able to depict Jewish people not as human beings but as entirely different forms of life? What disciplinary forces and movements shaped his bodily actions during the Nuremberg rallies, such that they had a profound impact on the behaviours and attitudes of others?

A further problem associated with a historiography which takes the founding subject as its basis is that it silences entire categories of people. Women, indigenous peoples and colonised peoples have all traditionally been marginalised within such historiography, at best understood as supporting actors or as players who have had history happen to them rather than being the makers of such history.

Accordingly, for Foucault, this kind of historiography is complicit with the practices of colonialism. Like colonialism it divides people into subjects and objects, active and passive, the colonising people who make history and develop knowledges, and the colonised people who are made the object of such history and knowledge. Thus the historian himself (traditionally most history was written by males) is positioned within the institutional practices and discourses of historiography as a colonial figure, able to penetrate deep into the various highways and byways of human affairs and make sense of it all through his magisterial gaze. Against such officially sanctioned historiographic knowledge Foucault develops the concept of 'subjugated knowledge'. This refers to the ways of knowing that have been buried under the dominant forms of knowledge that have developed in fields such as science, history and government as part of the colonial project. For example, native Americans may have forms of subjugated knowledge that make sense of the world in an entirely different way from that evident in western science. These forms of subjugated knowledge can help sustain a colonised people in their struggle against colonising forces.

Foucault's challenge to the way we make sense of history has significant implications for understanding the relations between different groups throughout the world today. The conflicts in the Middle East or the former Yugoslavia; the move by East Timorese people to claim independence from Indonesia: these issues and others have been shaped by historical forces. We can take the example of the dispute in the former Yugoslavia to show how Foucault's approach differs from others. The 'history of ideas' model of history would focus on the policies and motivations of leading figures, such as the architects of ethnic cleansing. A model that viewed history in terms of certain immutable laws would suggest that ancient ethnic tensions between Moslems, Slavs and other groups, which lay just below the surface, were released by the political and social instability brought on by the collapse of communism in the early 1990s. A Foucaultian approach would look at the emergence of certain discourses related to ethnicity, national identity, religious affiliation and militarism in this period, showing how these discourses positioned people in respect of others. A Foucaultian approach would also focus on the emergence of non-discursive forces that affected how people saw others not as they once had (as neighbours sharing a common territory), but as aliens encroaching on 'our' territory. So, rather than pointing to an historical inevitability underlying the Balkans dispute, a Foucaultian approach would seek to unravel these different and unpredictable factors, and demonstrate how they affected the way in which people spoke to and of, saw and acted towards one another.

This Foucaultian approach to history and geopolitical relations can help make sense of the role that discourse plays as a colonising force, and how it establishes relations between different groups of people. For example, in the aftermath of the Oklahoma bombing in 1995, when a large government office building (which also contained a child-care facility) was blown up by then-unknown terrorists, with substantial loss of life (including, of course, small children), much of the coverage focused on the shock that such terrorism should occur in the United States, which had, until then, been free of such atrocities. This discursive construction created a sense of a terrorist threat from outside, which led to a demonisation of Islamic fundamentalist groups—in a whole series of Hollywood movies (such as *True Lies* and *Clear and Present Danger*), Arab terrorists replaced the Soviets as the main menace to peace and freedom in the West. Of course the long history of terrorist activity in the United States (the dispossession of the native Americans, the slavery of Afro-Americans, the activities of the Ku Klux Klan) was conveniently ignored. It was then found that those responsible for the bombing included a Gulf War hero, whose attitudes drew upon these other 'terrorist' discourses that had played a constituent role in the settlement and development of the United States.

Geopolitical relations and postcolonialism

Geopolitical relations as they currently apply have been shaped by the emergence of discourses and forces connected with technology, migration patterns, media forms, the movement of ideologies and values, flows of money across global financial markets, and trade in a variety of products. Perhaps, most significantly, geopolitical relations have been shaped by the long period of Western colonisation of other parts of the earth. The writer Edward Said has noted (1978: 41) that direct European control over the earth's surface increased from 35 per cent in 1815 (the year marked by the Congress of Vienna which decided the shape of the world after the Napoleonic wars) to 85 per cent in 1914 (the year marked by the beginning of the First World War).

Such was the impact of this period of colonisation that it has become commonplace in many circles to describe the world today as postcolonial. That Americans and Australians speak English rather than another language; that significant numbers of Indians, Pakistanis and people from the West Indies choose to reside in Britain; that the music of the Beatles drew on influences as diverse as American blues and the sound of the Indian sitar: these circumstances and many others are a direct legacy of the colonial experience. And, although this colonial experience is over in the sense that many former colonised countries have now gained independence, the fall-out from colonialism will continue to impact on the world for many decades to come. In this context, Foucault has been identified as a significant postcolonial writer, because his ideas can help people come to terms with the implications of living in this postcolonial environment.

When Foucault wrote about colonialism, he rarely did so directly. For example, there are no books of his on the implications of the French colonial occupation of Indo-China, the Pacific and Africa, for example. Rather, he was interested in the way in which bodies were colonised by various forces, such as the disciplinary forces discussed in Chapter 4. Foucault was also interested in the way in which discourses played a colonising role in ordering experience, making sense of these experiences and distributing people within these orders. We might compare this with an explorer going out and colonising a piece of physical territory, claiming that territory as belonging to the home country, and establishing principles for settling that territory.

Using the terms coined by the writer Paul Virilio, we might say that Foucault was more concerned with endo-colonialism than with exo-colonialism. The prefix 'endo' means within or internal, while 'exo' means outside or external. Endo-colonialism refers to the way in which an internal territory is colonised, while exo-colonialism refers to the way in which other territories are colonised and brought within the control of an imperial power. These two processes meet in the age of western colonisation. Foucault's archaeologies and genealogies chart the way in which discourses and non-discursive forces, such as disciplinary power and the gaze, colonised bodies. For example, when people go to work in a factory, their bodies are colonised and manipulated in such a way that they become attuned to the rhythms of work and production that occur there. Similarly, schoolchildren are colonised by the discourses of the various academic disciplines that they are required to reproduce in their essays and tests. The endo-colonial forces helped produce a civil order and economic and administrative apparatuses recognisable as a nation-state. The nation-states that emerged in western Europe during the nineteenth century, having colonised their own people and territory, were equipped with the technologies, techniques and will to power to colonise other peoples and territories, resulting in the great period of colonial expansion. At the same time the task of pacifying, organising and regulating peoples and territories in the colonies provided colonial administrators and organisations with invaluable information and experience which they 'put to work' back home in Europe. As Franz Fanon pointed out, the apparatuses and methods associated with the 'treatment' of large groups of people (Jews, Slavs, homosexuals, leftists, gypsies) by the Nazis could be understood as colonialism being 'exported' back to Europe.

Governmentality and colonialism

In his studies of governmentality, Foucault noted how western governments became concerned with the problems involved in securing a territory and administering a population within this territory. The process of governmentality involved a move from government by the state to self-government, such that each member of the population might be equipped with various techniques that might make them effective and valued (and 'normal') members of that community. So each member of the community was meant to reflect upon their moral, productive/economic and bodily selves and adjust their behaviours in such a way as to produce themselves as proper members of that society. Those who violated such principles of propriety might then be excluded from that society and 'treated' in prisons, hospitals, asylums and other such places of confinement. We have seen how Foucault, throughout his career, provided histories of these places of confinement in order to show that, rather than simply being isolated from society, they helped shape social practice in a general way. For example, Foucault's discussion of the birth of the modern prison noted that the coercions, restraints, physical punishment, disciplinary training and work which took place there acted as a model for practices occurring throughout the social body, in institutions such as schools, workhouses and army barracks.

Foucault coined the term 'carceral continuum' to describe this process by which the carceral or punitive techniques of the prison gradually gained circulation throughout society as a whole. It is worth pointing out that this principle of carceral continuum circulated not only within the home country, but also became an important principle of the colonisation of other places in the eighteenth and nineteenth centuries. Indeed, the prison itself was one of the most important institutions involved in colonial practice. Certain western European countries regarded the colonies as places to which prisoners might be moved, believing that by removing them from the home country, their corrupting influence would also be removed.

One of the motivations for the American War of Independence in 1776 was settlers' dissatisfaction that British convicts were being sent to the American colonies. Having lost the War of Independence, Britain sought somewhere else to export its convicts and ease the burden on its overcrowded prisons. The Australian colonies were settled by Britain from 1788 as territories to house convicts. Similarly, the French used islands in the Pacific such as New Caledonia as dumping grounds for their convicts. In this way, the carceral continuum progressed from the home country to their colonial possessions.

Civilisation

The disciplinary work that went on in producing a temperate social order in the eighteenth and nineteenth centuries can be related to the project of civilisation. We tend to think of civilisation as a very old idea, emerging in the ancient world through societies in Greece, Rome and Egypt. For example, the Nile Delta is sometimes referred to as the 'cradle of civilisation'. In fact, the word 'civilisation' only began to enter into the language of western European countries from the middle of the eighteenth century. It refers to the process through which a civil social order was being created in these societies. This civilising process was based on the development of various disciplinary institutions and modes of governmentality, associated with schools, workhouses, family life and so forth. It involved inquiries and surveys into the conditions of life and moral values of the people living in the emerging urban slums associated with industrialisation.

For example, in England in the mid-nineteenth century Henry Mayhew conducted surveys of the living and moral conditions of people in the slum areas. Mayhew became a reporter of the underworld, able to distinguish various groups of criminals by the different terms through which they were identified. We see something similar in contemporary television series such as *NYPD Blue*, in which the detectives rely on working out characters' street names, and need to become literate in the special languages these groups use, in order to penetrate their networks.

The development of the popular press and sensational crime fiction owed something to the kind of work done by Henry Mayhew. The popular press helped develop a sense of community among the people in emerging urban areas, but also performed a policing role in respect of that community, focusing on the 'horrors' of violent crime and threats to security. We see this policing role still evident in the popular or tabloid press today. While such newspapers may feature photographs of topless girls, they will also devote much of their editorial space to stories depicting threats to the community's moral order. And the practices and people in these stories are denounced and vilified precisely because they are 'scandals' which offer contrary evidence to the community's claims to be civilised—they are represented as 'different from', and a threat to, our way of life. Popular current affairs television shows around the world offer an even better example of this—they actively seek out (and sometimes entrap) groups of people (shonky business people, the unemployed, single mothers, adolescents, drug users, welfare recipients) in the act of doing things (cheating little old ladies of their life savings, for instance) which show how 'we' are being 'ripped off'; how our civilised way of life is being undermined (by greed, corruption, drugs).

This civilising project had an important effect in shaping colonial practice in the rest of the world. On the one hand, it provided a moral justification for European colonisation. If the colonising countries could perceive themselves as being more civilised than the people in the countries they colonised then, rather than colonisation being seen as a naked act of aggression, it can seem morally justified, even righteous. The colonising project might be seen as bringing the light of civilisation to the dark and barbarous parts of the world. The Australian historian Manning Clark wrote as the first sentence in the first chapter in the first volume of his six-volume *A History of Australia*: 'Civilisation did not begin in Australia until the last quarter of the eighteenth century' (1962: 3). This is characteristic of much of the historiography written of European colonial practice at least up until the 1960s; it was concerned to depict the progress of civilisation as it supposedly emerged throughout the world. Indeed, one criterion of a civilised country was that it might write a history of itself.

Edward Said has applied Foucault's ideas to colonial practice in his famous book, *Orientalism* (1978). Said discusses how colonial practice was based on a construction of Oriental people as being less civilised than people in the West, and therefore needing to be colonised and governed by others. This discursive construction showed itself both in official governmental texts as well as popular culture texts such as the novels and poems of Rudyard Kipling. Drawing from Said's work, we can see how Orientalist discourses established a set of binary opposites, among which were:

Western people	Oriental people
Civilised	Barbarous
Active	Passive
Progressive	Backward
Subjects of knowledge	Objects of knowledge
Individuated	Unindividuated

In Chapter 4, we examined how disciplinary power worked according to a process of 'descending individualism', which distinguished people from others and marked them as individuals. School examinations, doctors' check-ups and measurements of a person's height, weight and any distinguishing characteristics: such techniques were characteristic of this process of descending individualism in which the techniques of individualisation tended to be exercised by people in positions of institutional power (doctors, teachers, psychologists and so forth) upon other people (patients, children, criminals and so forth). Such individualising techniques were part and parcel of the process of governmentality designed to administer and create a civil society in western Europe from the eighteenth century on.

In the context of colonial practice, there was a tendency to view colonised people as not being subject to these techniques of individualisation. Accordingly 'they' were understood as being part of a mass, or horde, and lacking the values that marked 'us' as members of a civilised society. For example, the film *Gunga Din* (1939), based on a story by Rudyard Kipling, depicts strongly individuated British soldiers fighting a horde of Indian 'natives' who are depicted as being underhand and sneaky in their methods of fighting. This distinction between strongly individualised westerners and unindividuated Oriental people is still evident in films like *True Lies* (1994) or *The Siege* (1998). In *True Lies*, the strongly individuated American hero, Arnold Schwarzenegger, battles a crazed fundamentalist Islamic group, the Crimson Jihad, whose members are presented as fanatical and mindless, and manipulated by their leader. A similar theme is depicted in Bruce Willis' *The Siege*, where Middle-Eastern terrorists are herded into detention camps after they bomb New York City; an approach that has offended American Muslims and Arabs.

Colonial gaze

These distinctions between western and Oriental people can be linked to the concept of a 'colonial gaze'. We discussed in Chapter 4 how techniques of surveillance were a fundamental part of the mechanism of disciplinary power. We are produced as being constantly subject to the gaze of others and ourselves, and our behaviour, speech, body shape and moral attitudes are constantly being monitored. These techniques of surveillance played an important role in colonial rule. The forms of knowledge that were produced about colonised people were a means of making them the object of the colonisers' surveillance. The film *Gunga Din* draws upon this logic of surveillance by depicting the British as occupying open space in the full light of day, while the Indian characters are depicted sneaking around in shadows. There is a perceived need, then, to monitor closely the Indian natives' behaviours and attitudes, as they are not to be trusted. And the same kind of logic is displayed in the way contemporary popular films treat the threat of terrorism. In the film *Patriot Games*, for example, Irish and Arabic terrorists, who move about and do their deeds at night, are identified, targeted and destroyed by high-tech, infra-red military spying devices and weaponry which effectively removes the protection offered by darkness. The whole world, according to this scenario, can be monitored, to the smallest detail, day or night, by spy satellites.

A similar logic is evident today in western constructions of Islamic people. It was interesting that during the Gulf War in 1991, the military was at pains to restrict media access to information, but was happy to release footage of successful bombing raids, which seemed to suggest that the Allied forces' surveillance of Baghdad was so complete and expert that it could guide a bomb through a minute opening to its target.

Heterotopia

Evident in the clash of cultures in colonial and postcolonial contexts is Foucault's concept of heterotopia. Heterotopia refers to the way in which different spaces can come into contact with other spaces that seem to bear no relation to them. The experience of heterotopia disposes people to wonder which world they are in. An example is the way in which British colonial figures in India established gentlemen's clubs along the lines of those found in London, but which bore no relationship to the conditions of life as experienced by people in India. Thus a space within India was fitted out and made British—a space where people drank gin and tonic, dressed in evening suits, read the *Times* and played cricket (not all at the same time). This logic provides the impetus for controlling and regulating the movements of people throughout the space of a colonised country. The colonised people must be restricted from entering the space of the colonial power. Indeed, the power to regulate the movements through space of others was an integral element in the practice of colonialism. In extreme cases, this power led to the development of apartheid in South Africa and the establishment of concentration camps to confine colonised others.

We can see this concern with the regulation of space in contemporary popular culture in films such as *The Lion King*. This film portrays the lions in colonial terms as the natural and proper rulers of the jungle, who are able to survey their territory from the panoptic position of a rock overlooking their kingdom. In the context of a contemporary world in which the movement of goods, information and people throughout the globe has become both more rapid and vastly more voluminous, the sense of living in a heterotopic world of an infinity of different and often conflicting spaces can produce a crisis of identity. Films like *The Lion King* can tap into this anxiety and offer the consolation of a world where the division and control of space seems natural and proper.

The principle of heterotopia is also evident in the film *Titanic*, where the privileged world of the rich and upper classes is literally superimposed on the world of the characters who travel in steerage class. While the regulation of space within the ship was designed to keep these worlds apart (the Leonardo di Caprio and Kate Winslet characters cross this spatial divide), it is the collision with the other natural world of the iceberg which brings these different social worlds into open conflict.

A further example is the popularity of British television shows such as *Heartbeat*, *Hamish Macbeth* and *Ballykissangel*, which set their stories in rural spaces populated by 'good, simple folk', and which are more or less cut off from urban and city spaces, and largely devoid of all the problems or intrusions (drugs, corruption, violence, scandals, migrants) that characterise the city. The narrative of these shows usually revolves around some kind of intrusion of outside ways or people (bureaucracy, government policy, gangsters), and the coming together of the community to overcome those intrusions, and thus maintain the 'sanctity' of this space, and their control over their 'natural' way of life.

Foucault's ideas challenge the basis of this 'natural' and 'proper' control. For the heterotopic anxiety gives rise to various technologies which are charged with policing the division of space, all of which have significant consequences for the way in which people make sense of themselves and the worlds through which they move.

Conclusion

In this chapter we have discussed the implications of Foucault's work for understanding the practice of history and geopolitical relations within both a colonial and postcolonial context. This is important because:

- Foucault's approach critiques those schools of history which focus on the ideas of influential people or identify underlying laws governing the development of history;
- Foucault shows how discursive and non-discursive forces shape people's attitudes and actions as they move across the various spaces that make up their lives. These historical forces can be broken down into a series of events that can be distinguished from one another.

For Foucault, then, the role of his archaeological and genealogical studies is to equip readers with the critical tools to understand how their being has been fashioned by historical forces, such that they might be able to intervene in this fashioning. How people might do this, and with what results, are explored in the final three chapters of this book.

Further reading

Bhabha, Homi 1994, *The Location of Culture*, Routledge, London, see 'Introduction'

Certeau, Michel de 1988, *The Writing of History*, Columbia University Press, New York, see Chapter 2

Said, Edward 1978, *Orientalism*, Penguin, Harmondsworth, see Chapter 1

Stoler, Ann 1995, *Race and the Education of Desire*, Duke University Press, Durham, see Chapters 1, 2, 3

Young, Robert 1990, *White Mythologies: Writing History and the West*, Routledge, London, see Chapter 1

8

The ethical subject

Technologies of the self

> The goal of my work during the last twenty years has
> not been to analyze the phenomenon of power, nor
> to elaborate the foundations of such an analysis. My
> objective, instead, has been to create a history of the
> different modes by which, in our culture, human beings
> are made subjects. (Foucault 1984b: 7)

In this final section of the book we look at Foucault's response
to the question of what (or who) is 'the subject'. Foucault's
ideas on the subject changed throughout his career. We will
describe some of the more important moves, and suggest how
we can use his theories to make sense of the relations between
individuals and the societies in which they live.

To do this, we need to recall sections of the earlier chapters
which set out the theoretical background on which Foucault's
work is built, and from which it departs. His early work,
which largely depends on notions taken from Nietzsche,
begins with the idea that the subject is 'dead' because, rather
than being the source of meaning, it is produced by discourses, institutions and relations of power. What this means
is that people are not free agents who make their own meanings and control their lives; rather, they have their lives,
thoughts and activities 'scripted' for them by social forces and

institutions (such as schools, the media and advertising). In his later work, however, Foucault considers the ways in which people—what he calls 'subjects'—are active in 'crafting' or negotiating their identity.

We will explore these ideas over the next three chapters. In this chapter we outline the foundations of Foucault's work in this area, and focus on his notion that the self is created or crafted through what he calls 'technologies of the self'. In the following chapter we discuss the way in which subjectivity ties in with sexuality and focus on his concept of 'micropower'. In the final chapter we will pick up on his later work on the subject, particularly his notion that life should be lived and performed as a work of art.

The idea of the subject

From an everyday point of view, 'the subject' seems to be a very straightforward concept—we all know what a person is, or at least we think we do. From a political point of view, it is an abstract and universal 'thing', the 'I' who is referred to in national constitutions, and has a range of rights and responsibilities—to vote, to work, to raise children, to bear arms (in the United States), to be tried by peers and, more generally, to be a member of civic society. On a personal level, the subject is simply any one and all of us, a particular person who lives within a social environment, and who has certain qualities. This person may be tall, obese, quick-tempered, or good at crossword puzzles. She or he explains her or his personality in terms of 'just being made this way', as though there were a real inner core, inevitable and unchangeable, regardless of changes in cultural contexts or historical periods. In other words, 'the subject' is both a political entity—the person who belongs to the community and its systems of government— and a specific identity owned by the self.

For philosophy though, who and what the subject is has never been either simple or obvious. The question of how we can understand the self has, for thousands of years, been a central issue for philosophy. And it is an important question, because determining who and what the subject is determines how the subject should be treated, and should treat others. Foucault explores this question by studying and analysing the approaches taken by western philosophy from the ancient Greek times to the present and, in the process, he brings something new to our understandings of the self. This interest in the subject is found throughout his writings: from early works such as *The Order of Things* where he examines how, in particular historical moments, people become objects of knowledge, to his last series, the *History of Sexuality*, where he examines how people constitute themselves, his work deals with the emergence of what he calls 'man', or the subject, in history and in discourse. As we have seen already in the sections on knowledge and power, he takes an 'archaeological' approach, examining the various ways in which the self has been understood differently through history. He identifies, in particular historical moments, the dominant understandings of the subject which are shared by philosophy, education, commercial and governmental institutions, and people in their everyday lives.

By analysing these different understandings of the subject, Foucault shows that the subject is not natural, but takes on different forms in different historical periods. In other words, rather than being the free and active organisers of society, we are products of discourses and power relations, and take on different characteristics according to the range of subject positions that are possible in our socio-historical context. And because social understandings of the subject change across history, the subject cannot be self-aware of this process. To make sense of this, we will trace some major themes in philosophy's understandings of the subject, and some of the ways in which Foucault makes use of them.

On becoming a subject

Foucault begins by reading the ancient Graeco-Roman and early Christian philosophers on 'the self'. The main idea they shared—though they defined the terms somewhat differently—was that the self could be perfected, and that only those who were striving to perfect themselves could have access to rationality and truth. The attempt to 'perfect the self' involved the use of various regulatory practices (or 'technologies of the self'), including the repeated experience of struggling to overcome those things that threatened self-mastery. Foucault quotes Antiphon the Sophist to the effect that 'He is not wise who has not tried the ugly and the bad; for then there is nothing he has conquered and nothing that would enable him to assert that he is virtuous' (Foucault 1986b: 66). A comical version of this idea occurs in the film *Monty Python and the Search for the Holy Grail*, where a knight searching for the Grail comes upon the Castle of the Nymphomaniacs. He wants to stay there, but his companions, fearing that he will fail to maintain his vow of chastity, stop him. He is dragged away, screaming 'Let me stay and resist temptation'.

A more modern example of this idea occurs in the film *Heathers*, where a teenage girl (played by Winona Ryder) is tempted by a new boy in the school (Christian Slater) to join him in giving full rein to their desires—which involves murdering all the nasty and unpleasant members of their class. Although eliminating the 'nasties', and getting away with it (the murders are made to look like suicides), is exhilarating for Ryder's character, she ends up rejecting (that is, overcoming) the temptation to act as judge, jury and executioner of her classmates. She masters her desires—which supposedly (in the film) makes her a better person. Why? Because she meets her devils (Christian Slater is closely identified with the devil) and defeats them/him.

By the Classical age (from the late sixteenth century), scientific reason was considered a more important means for discovering 'the truth' about things than the struggle for self-mastery. This was because, by this period, science was fairly well established as a discipline capable of producing a set of categories for ordering and explaining the world. Human beings were not considered 'subjects' as we now understand the term; instead, they were classified as a genus or species—along with all other forms of life. And because humans weren't considered to be essentially different from other life forms, there was no idea of a separate 'human nature'.

It was not until the seventeenth century that the subject emerged both as an object of scientific curiosity and, in what constituted a major scientific and philosophical change (replacing God, in a sense), as the source of scientific reason. Along with the emergence of Descartes' famous *cogito, ergo sum* ('I think, therefore I am'), the idea of human reason took the place of the ancient search for knowledge-through-purity, or the more recent approach of classifying humans as a category of nature. Scientists came to understand people as being essentially different from plants, rocks and animals. The human subject was now understood to be both site and founder of knowledge and reason.

Immanuel Kant (1724–1804), a German philosopher considered by many to be the most influential thinker of modern times, made some of the most important contributions to this changing view. He claimed that the material world is fundamentally unknowable, and exists for us only as the raw material of sensations. Consequently, he argued, reason must be the final authority for moral judgements or actions, and individuals must be free to govern themselves and to obey the laws of nature and society as they are revealed by reason. From this comes his famous 'categorical imperative', which dictates that a course of action must be followed because of its rightness and necessity. In other words, the subject is both free and subjected—free to choose, but with only one 'right' choice available—the 'choice' of the 'duty' that involves obeying reason.

Let's go back to the example of the film *Heathers*. The Winona Ryder character, in eliminating all the 'nasties' in her school, was acting in terms of her desires, rather than in terms of her reason. Yes, the nasties were bullying other students, but Ryder acted out of her own personal loathing of them, and out of a desire to revenge herself upon them (they had trashed her as well). At the end of the film, after she has rejected the devil and his temptations (Christian Slater and his violence), she has been transformed. From now on, she will act in the interests of the whole community, particularly the powerless and the weak. Her final words are 'There's a new sheriff in town'—which means that Ryder has accepted her duty, and will act to ensure that reason, not power, prevails within the school community.

Of course there is one small problem with Kant's categorical imperative—who decides what is reason, or what is in the best interests of everyone? The people who ran Pol Pot's death camps, for instance, claimed to be doing their duty, and acting according to the dictates of reason—which involved, as far as they were concerned, (eventually) making the world a better place for all people. We will return to this problem in our later discussion of Foucault's notion of an ethics of the self.

Freedom and the subject

The attempt to judge whether individuals are either free subjects or subjected to the control or regulation of power exposes a central paradox of Western philosophy's thinking about human subjectivity and freedom. One position is that what we are and do is based on an inevitability (divine will, predestination, or just being born a particular type of person). The other position is that we are assumed to be capable of choosing actions that are 'right' according to a final and unchanging standard—that is, reason. These mutually contradictory views have had to coexist in philosophy, but have been wrestled over in philosophical and religious debates. Judas, for instance, was often the 'text' used to discuss this issue, because if he was 'born like that', a betrayer and destined to betray Christ, how could he have refused that destiny? And, having acted in accordance with his (human) nature and with what he was destined to do, how can we hold him responsible for his inevitable betrayal? All of which begs the question: what do we mean when we talk about 'human nature'?

By the late nineteenth century, the 'human sciences'—which incorporates philosophy, sociology, psychology, criminology, economics and so on, as well as the 'hard sciences' such as medicine and psychiatry—began paying serious attention to human nature, which meant producing systems of classification which defined who could be a subject, the conditions for subjectivity, and what it means to be a subject. Many different ways of viewing individuals and their relations with others were developed and articulated. Some took a rather cynical view of the status of the relation between the self and the community. Freud, for instance, rejected the idea of the free or responsible self, describing the subject as something which is driven and managed by desire, and which acquires characteristics by virtue of external influences—the family in particular. Marxist writers too argued that the subject was neither natural nor free, but existed only when it was 'interpellated' (or called up) by powerful social institutions.

What do we mean by interpellation? Think of how a person watching television tends to identify with ideas and characteristics that are promoted as good, desirable or right. In the BBC police series *The Bill*, for instance, the police are usually shown as brave, caring, hard working and (mostly) honest, while the criminals are generally treated less sympathetically (they are usually nasty, lazy and brutal). As we watch the show unfold, it 'calls us up' by engaging our sympathies with the police—we are like them, we believe in the things they do, in a similar situation we would act like them. The show becomes, in a sense, a mirror which tells us what a 'good' subjectivity is, and gives us a model to emulate. We 'become' the subjectivity that the producers of the series provide for us.

Foucault picks up on aspects of both Freudian and Marxist schools of thought, and argues that the subject can't pre-exist the social order, or be the source of meaning, because it is itself constituted by dominant social rules. Who and what the self is understood to be, and how the self interacts with others, varies significantly over history and between cultures. From this comes Foucault's famous declaration of the 'death of the subject':

> As the archaeology of our thought easily shows, man is an invention of recent date. And one perhaps nearing its end. If those arrangements were to disappear as they appeared, if some event of which we can at the moment do no more than sense the possibility . . . were to cause them to crumble, as the ground of Classical thought did . . . then one can certainly wager that man would be erased, like a face drawn in sand at the edge of the sea. (1973: 387)

Interestingly, there is already plenty of evidence, scattered through contemporary culture, to back up Foucault's 'prophecy' about the disappearance of 'man'. Popular cultural forms such as films, novels and Japanese *manga* comics are full of examples of futuristic (and, in some cases, contemporary) societies dominated or populated by 'cyborgs'—part human, part machine. Films such as *Bladerunner, Terminator, Robocop* and *The Matrix*, the novels of Phillip K. Dick and William Gibson, and *manga* comics such as *Akira*, all accept the extinction of the 'pure human'—what Foucault calls 'man'—and its replacement by something that is as much a walking, talking machine driven by contrary and contradictory personalities, urges and logics. In *Robocop*, Murphy's actions are literally programmed into him, but his dreams help him to seek out and maintain a connection with his human past. On a more mundane level, in our contemporary world most of us are 'artificial' or part-machine in some way, either because we rely on prosthetics (eyes, teeth, legs, hips, breasts, buttocks, heart, hair), or because we are connected to machines for much of the time (computers, for instance).

For Foucault, our notion of the 'human being' is not inevitable; it is historical. People do not have natural and unchanging characteristics. Rather, we are produced out of a network of discourses, institutions and relations, and always liable to change according to the circumstances. So, although we think of ourselves as unified, concrete individuals with certain unchanging qualities, in fact we are a number of different people: the person we are at home is not fully identical with the one at work, facing a law suit or spending time with a pet or a lover (or both). The kind of subject or person we are in different places and times depends on the rules, discourses and ideas in a culture which determine what can be said, thought and done, and on the social and historical context in which we live. For instance, a man might work in a lowly position in an office, and because he has no status, he behaves in a nervous and self-effacing manner. However, on the squash court, as the Zambian All-Comers undisputed champion for the last twenty years, he is quite different—aggressive, tough, confident—even arrogant. Which is the 'real' subjectivity here? Neither—and both. It just depends on which context the person is in.

Biopolitics

For the early Foucault, subjectivity is also shaped by the way in which individuals' bodies are acted upon by disciplinary technologies. The body is central to the question of who the self is, because individuals are classified in terms of their bodies and their bodily function. Women, for instance, generally have a different experience of subjectivity than do men; the subjectivity of children or the very old is different from that of young people; race, ethnicity, physical appearance and health all contribute to how we see ourselves and are seen by others. Think of how the images of young and incredibly thin women that appear in magazines predispose girls to think well of themselves only if they can replicate that shape—despite the fact that it is unhealthy and unrealistic (very few people are actually that shape, even the models, whose photographs are often 'doctored').

Foucault developed these ideas by examining how the body is managed, organised and disciplined in institutions such as prisons, schools or hospitals. The term he developed to discuss the relation between the human body and institutions of power is biopolitics. This term provides ways of understanding how and why government institutions are interested in managing human bodies, an interest that stems from the eighteenth century when the idea of 'population' first emerged. In earlier chapters we have seen some of the techniques used by the state to regulate—or discipline—their subjects. Now with the practice of biopolitics the state also took on the responsibility of managing the population as a resource. Governments produced the body, in their discourses, as an object of social concern, and used tools like social policy to produce particular types of populations. Health policy, for instance, ensures we are fit and well, and thus able to contribute to the workforce; policies that proscribe homosexuality ensure that we use our sexual energy to produce babies who will become new subjects of the state, and new workers and consumers. In other words, people's physical bodies were seen as resources available to meet the interests of the state.

Foucault argues that the policies developed by disciplinary sites establish what he calls 'discursive norms'. In the nineteenth century in Britain, for instance, there were a number of groups and individuals involved in interventions designed to try to save people from alcoholism, and give them some kind of basic education. Now, on one level this was done for humanitarian reasons, but another, in some ways more important, reason was that drunk and uneducated workers weren't very productive. In other words, it was good business (both for factory owners and the state) to keep the parents sober, and send their children to school. The idea of the sober, literate factory worker became the 'discursive norm'. Mothers were then enlisted, through a series of institutional discourses (from the church, the growing education and health systems, and government policies directed, for instance, at schooling or employment standards) to more or less 'police' this norm—they were expected to keep an eye on both their husbands and their children, to make sure that they were doing 'the right thing'.

Such practices require systems of classification which sort out what the standards are, who fits the standards, and who can be considered a genuine subject. They also depend on a series of coercive technologies and practices which ensure that only particular kinds of individuals are named as 'normal', and hence as subjects. We can see this in the many ways in which European governments and communities have classified and treated insane people. In the early Middle Ages—around the thirteenth century—madness was classified as a vice rather than a condition or a category, and insane people were imprisoned or beaten, sometimes left to their own resources, or even expelled from their communities (though in some cases they were cared for by their communities). By the Classical period, insanity was no longer considered a vice, but the insane were now considered to be members of a different class of human being. They were often housed in boats and set loose to drift along European canals and rivers, and so were simultaneously part of, and excluded from, society. By the eighteenth century, madness was understood to be a condition that was in opposition to reason, and various forms of madness were identified and classified. It was during this period that great houses of confinement were established, not only for the mad but also for the poor and the sick. This, which Foucault connects to the economic crisis that was then affecting all Europe, was a way of separating the mad and the unemployable from society at large, and also of getting some work out of them: these houses were also places of production. The insane, of course, were rarely well enough to work effectively, reliably or in a disciplined manner, and so were now also classified as socially useless, and hence as shameful, as creatures that should be hidden away. And, certainly, the insane continue to be seen as potential threats to the community. The Thatcher government's decision in the 1980s to empty asylums was seen as a scandal not only because it meant that the government was no longer prepared to take responsibility for the insane, but also because it put the mad back amongst 'us', the 'real' (reasonable and reasoning) human beings.

These examples of the 'production of subjectivity' (the mad, the insane, the pervert, the outcast) come about by way of what Foucault calls technologies of classifying, disciplining, analysing and normalising; and they depend to a large extent on the process of naming. Human beings across cultures and across history have named themselves, both as communities and as individuals, and have denied names—and hence 'real' subjectivity—to slaves and other non-people. So an important precondition for being truly human is having a name which denotes an identity that is distinct from everyone else. For people in western cultures, the possibility of losing our particular identities (our subjectivity) is the stuff of psychosis or horror. We can find an example of this horror in popular culture: one of the worst enemies in the *Star Trek* series is 'the Borg', a 'collective consciousness' which rampages across the universe assimilating everyone into itself, and destroying any trace of individual character. For a real life example, we only have to think of the way in which the Third Reich stripped the inmates of its concentration camps of their names, and tattooed them with numbers. This made them non-human—and therefore easy to abuse and kill. Our personal names distinguish us from everyone and everything else, and thus allow us to claim an identity as a unique subject. So we become subjects by naming ourselves as particular individuals, and as the occupiers of particular sets of subject positions (such as mother, daughter, worker).

The naming process also works to make us subjects by naming and identifying what we are not (such as mad, old, or sick)—that is, through technologies of differentiation. Those who are not-subjects are those who fail to meet the conditions defined as normal—because they are mad, old or sick, for instance. It is, in the first instance, these others, these not-subjects or not-quite-subjects, who are locked up in prisons or mental clinics, trapped in poverty on pensions, numbed by medication, and shamed in public. These sorts of practices force human beings to work on themselves in order to meet and comply with the models normalised by the individual's culture, which they exchange for the promise of subject status (that is, acceptance as normal human beings).

This sort of argument has led many commentators and critics to complain that Foucault considers human beings to be no more than 'docile bodies'. For Foucault, though, the self is not just the raw material—the docile body—which is worked on by discourses, institutions and power relations. Rather, we are capable of a moral or an ethical dimension. Though we may be the effects of power relations, we are not helpless objects formed and moved by power, but individuals constituted as subjects by governmental practices of power and normalisation, and we can choose to respond to, or resist, these practices. An example, here, is of schoolchildren: they are placed in an institution with strict codes, rules, regulations, imperatives and ideas of subjectivity that they are meant to conform to—but rarely do. And the students who do readily conform to the models of 'good subjectivity' are invariably ostracised by their peers—they are teacher's pet, or brownnosers, or geeks. They are often unpopular precisely because they do what they're supposed to. Although schools may work to produce 'docile bodies', they are just as likely to produce rebels.

Technologies of the self

This idea that individuals are (potentially) active agents capable of working on the self leads us to Foucault's later work in this area. In his three-volume *History of Sexuality*, and especially in the third volume, *The Care of the Self*, Foucault picks up the idea of an ethics of the self—so central to ancient Graeco-Roman, Christian and Enlightenment thought—to suggest ways of living in the world. To examine this part of his work, we need to look at what he calls 'technologies of the self'.

Technologies of the self are a series of techniques that allow individuals to work on themselves by regulating their bodies, their thoughts and their conduct. These processes, Foucault argues, are offered to us as avenues through which we can achieve a degree of perfection, happiness, purity and wisdom. As he writes in *The History of Sexuality*, technologies of the self are ways of attempting to live the truth, tell the truth, and be changed by the truth. One of the important technologies of the self is self-knowledge: 'knowing the self' involves determining the truth about the self, because only in knowing this truth can we work on ourselves to achieve perfectibility. This notion of self-knowledge was central to technologies of self-formation in Graeco-Roman and early Christian philosophies and practices, where the instruction, 'take care of yourself', actually meant 'know yourself'.

Foucault identifies three main technologies of the self, or techniques for achieving subjectivity in western cultural history, all of which involve self-examination. The first, which he terms Senecan, is a series of techniques which allows us to examine how our thoughts tie in with the rules of society. The second, early Christian hermeneutics, was concerned with understanding the relations between our inner thoughts and our inner impurity. And finally there is the Cartesian mode, which examines the extent to which our thoughts correspond to reality. Although they have different logics, values and goals, all three emphasise the need to verbalise our thoughts as a way of examining and knowing the self. In Graeco-Roman writings individuals were encouraged to keep a journal, or to tell the secrets of the self to a respected friend. With the emergence of Christianity, subjectivity depended on renouncing the self in an attempt to constitute a new self, but the technology of verbalising—in prayer and confession—remained important. And it still is, in many ways: medicine, psychiatry and psychology all encourage us to find the truth of our physical or mental well-being by talking it out with professionals. In the legal institution, at schools and university, in our sexual relations, in the family and on Oprah Winfrey's show, this practice of verbalising is so thoroughly entrenched that a whole series of industries has sprung up to exploit it. Indeed, it has become part of the natural order of truth and reality: the idea that we can, by examining our conscience and confessing our thoughts and deeds, find the truth about ourselves.

The point of the technologies of the self for the ancients and in the Christian era was to ensure that individual subjects could become competent to take up a position within the society that would not harm others, and that, through the exercise of 'proper' relations, would benefit the community as a whole. In other words, it was the duty of the individual to try to perfect the self—not only for self-improvement, but for the betterment of society. Because of this, caring for the self was seen as ethical, not selfish: its goal was to achieve a complete and full life for the individual and, in the process, for the community.

Ethics and the self

But the notion of ethics is highly problematic. We are living at the end of a century during which any stable and permanent truths which we could use as the basis for an ethics have been severely shaken. Religion, which for centuries was the final judge of truth and meaning, is no longer in a position where its truths are widely shared, and no other institution or belief system, in the West at least, has risen to take its place as an overall guarantor of truth. Despite this absence, we typically try to find a point of truth on which to construct a life and an identity. And although earlier discursive modes may have been forgotten or have lost their power, our sense of morals and ethics are still influenced by old belief systems: as Gilles Deleuze writes, 'we continue to produce ourselves as a subject on the basis of old modes which do not correspond to our problems' (1988: 107). To go back to the example of the Third Reich, historians and commentators have puzzled over why so many European Jews went like sheep to their deaths. One answer offered is that for many of them, their subjectivity was still based on the idea of religion—that their God would take care of them—and that Jewish society was organised in terms of the rule of law, justice and truth. Accordingly, they produced themselves as subjects in relation to the state in these terms, despite the fact that the rule of law was dedicated to killing Jews, there was no justice and their 'truth' was overruled.

All the same, Foucault does argue that the practice of an ethics can be used as a technique for resisting oppression and power. For Foucault, the self does not emerge in society naturally. Rather, it is constituted through 'a game of truth, relations of power, and forms of relation to oneself and to others' (1998: 117); that is to say, the self is tied up with ethics, political action and knowledge. We cannot know the truth about ourselves, because there is no truth to know, simply a series of practices that make up the self. Nor can we escape the regulatory institutions and discourses in which we are produced. But we can identify them (or at least some of them), and identify our own practices of the self, and from this basis of knowledge, formulate tactics by which we can live in the world. So, while Foucault doesn't accept the idea of a 'true self', he insists that we can work on ourselves (our selves) to reinvent ourselves as subjects better fitted for living with the self and with others. Again the example from *Heathers* is appropriate here—Winona Ryder rejected both the pressures to conform to power (which meant treating weak and unfashionable people badly), and the desire to 'wipe out' everybody she didn't like. At the end of the film she reinvents herself as her own self, not somebody else's.

Conclusion

In this chapter we have looked at Foucault's writings on who 'the subject' is, and how we can recognise ourselves and others as subjects. We outlined his writings on:

- the 'commonsense', the philosophical, and general historical ideas of 'the subject';
- the development of discourses of freedom and responsibility that circulate around the subject, especially biopolitics;

- technologies of the self, such as self-knowledge, verbalis-ation and self-improvement.

This leads us to two major issues. The first, which we will examine in the following chapter, concerns the grounds of morality in relationships, and like Foucault, we will deal with this by looking at the place of sexuality and how it ties in to the idea of the subject. The second issue is about establishing an ethics of existence in the absence of any final guarantor of truth, and in the last chapter we will trace Foucault's response, which is to substitute for morality an aesthetics of existence: the production of the self as a work of art.

Further reading

Butler, Judith 1997b, *The Psychic Life of Power*, Stanford University Press, Stanford, see Chapter 3

McNay, Lois 1994, *Foucault: A Critical Introduction*, Continuum, New York, see Chapter 4

Ransom, John 1997, *Foucault's Discipline: The Politics of Subjectivity*, Duke University Press, Durham and London, 1997, see Chapter 6

9

The sexual subject

Despite Foucault's own insistence in interviews that sex is boring, he is widely known as a writer on sex and sexuality. His three-volume *History of Sexuality* provides an impressive and sweeping map of attitudes to sexuality in several major historical periods. Interestingly, it has very little to say about sex as such, but instead closely examines the history of thought on sex and sexuality, and the discourses on sex which are used to manage populations. So, for Foucault, sex is less about bodies, erotics and desire than it is about technologies of government and technologies of the self. And this intimate association with technologies, and hence with the networks of power and knowledge that organise societies, is the reason that he considers 'boring' sex to be worth studying.

An important aspect of sex and sexuality is the macro-level issue of how social relations should be organised, and of what constitutes ethical behaviour, in sex and more generally in family or social situations. But Foucault's most focused attention goes to the way in which the discourses and technologies on sex produce categories of sexual practices and sexual identity by which we are marked as particular kinds of subjects (normal or deviant, for instance). This notion of subjectivity is based on the body because the types of body we possess (old/young, male/female, gorgeous/needs some work) mark us as particular types of individuals (desirable, invisible, disgusting, irrelevant). And the way in which we inhabit these bodies, and live out our (sexual) identities, shapes the type of life we can expect to live, and the various relationships in which we will engage. So although the ethics and the rules of social and sexual conduct may differ dramatically across history and cultures, sexual discourses—on practices, identity, or body type—contribute significantly to how societies establish the 'truth' of the subject, and the norms for the relations that subjects should have with themselves and others.

There are plenty of examples in popular culture where a 'plain Jane' type of character (glasses, conservative clothes, dull hair-do, prudish, passive or meek body language, softly spoken) is suddenly transformed—usually when a man intervenes and 'makes her over' or, in the case of one recent advertisement, when she changes her shampoo—into a dynamic, glamorous, sexually assertive 'tiger'. The 'truth' of her subjectivity changes with her sexuality, or at least her current 'performance' of sexuality. Of course that performance of sexuality—which is like a script which she reads and acts out—does in fact change the kind of person or subject she is, and how she relates to others, but it has nothing to do with liberating her 'true self'. She is simply being 'written' by different discourses of sexuality and subjectivity.

In this chapter we will first examine some of the dominant discourses, especially the ways in which they change with historical and cultural changes, and how they are used to organise people. Then we will briefly look at the connections between the body and the subject, because although we will be discussing sex as a social construct, and an effect of power and knowledge, it is still undeniably a bodily function. Foucault uses the term 'micro-power' to explain how discourses 'write' the body, or shape the ways in which bodies are understood and function. As these discourses change across history, so too does the body—or rather, the way in which we understand and code our bodily functions—changes. To make sense of this we will look at the technologies used to manage the body, and the relation between the body and the rational, self-governing subject. These technologies are an aspect of whatever passes, in a particular context, for morality and ethics and, in the last part of this chapter, we look at sexual ethics and outline Foucault's view that this is one of the ways in which people become subjects—members of society.

Sex *vs* sexuality

Although we tend to use the words 'sex' and 'sexuality' as though they mean more or less the same thing, Foucault makes a distinction between them. 'Sex', for Foucault, is a physical act that is also a 'family matter'—it is through sex that we are produced as individuals who belong to a network of relations and alliances, the network in which family property and family values are transferred, and the network in which we emerge as particular subjects—subjects with names and histories. 'Sexuality', by contrast, is an 'individual matter'—involving our personal desires, fantasies, pleasures—and also a matter of discourse and governmentality. It is here that norms and standards are established and policed, and it is here that we come to understand the relationship between our sexuality and our society's rules. This does not mean that sex is something 'real' and sexuality simply an arrangement of discourses and structures of power. Both are 'real'—sex in its effects on the physical body, and sexuality in its effects on the social body (in that it materialises beliefs and practices). Both are also cultural—sex because the ways in which we perform sexually are established by dominant discourses, and sexuality, because it is constructed in particular social and historical contexts. For the ancient Greeks, for instance, homosexuality was not just acceptable but, at certain periods, was actually understood as one of the highest forms of expression. Today, in many parts of the world, homosexuals are tried and imprisoned, or beaten and murdered. So, while in antiquity the physical sexual act may have involved the same body parts and movements as it does for us today, its meanings and its rules—how you do it, where and with whom, how you talk about it—were very different from the way in which we now understand and experience those same body parts and movements.

In short, sex and sexuality together comprise a set of practices, behaviours, rules and knowledges by which we produce ourselves, and are produced, as 'knowing'—ethical, social and juridical—subjects. It is a human experience that affects and involves the body (How does—and how should—my body perform? What are the mechanics of sex?), desires (What turns me on?), forms of knowledge (How do I 'do' sex? What does it mean?), fears (What do I risk by having sex here and now, with this person, in this way?) and social rules (What sort of sex is the right sort? If someone finds out what I'm doing, will I be punished?). So sex is far more than a way of procreating, or even a way of experiencing pleasure. Rather, it is tied up with meanings and power; it is a form of knowledge as well as a physical activity; and it involves one's relation to the self as much as one's relations with others.

Sexual discourse

Foucault's *History of Sexuality* looks at these two important relations (to the self and to others) by charting social and governmental discourses on sexuality from antiquity, through the Middle Ages in Europe, to the Victorian age when modern sexuality first emerges. He details the ways in which views ('truths') on sexuality—a set of truths, understandings and practices—change across cultures, and the different sorts of rules it has received during these periods. This 'archaeology of sex' problematises the way in which we understand sex and engage in it and other social activities—in fact, the way we live in general—because it shows that things are not 'just the way they are'. Rather, they are made the way they are by social norms and practices, by the institutions and discourses that regulate our behaviour, and by the way we regulate ourselves. And what this means is that it is always possible to regulate ourselves in different ways, to live otherwise.

Certainly sexuality has been 'otherwise' across these centuries. For an example of this, we can think about the status of paedophilia. During the late 1990s, the media regularly presented 'shocking' and 'scandalous' accounts of paedophilia and, in 1998, reported that Interpol had mounted a major operation to trap 'cyberspace paedophiles'—an Internet club whose members swapped pornographic photographs of children. Although a co-ordinated series of raids in twelve countries netted only a few dozen of its members, it was hailed as a major and an important success in the battle against perversion. Whatever we may think about this use of resources given the other dangers faced by children—hunger, war, over-work, domestic violence—the scale of the project and, presumably, its cost signals just how seriously Interpol, and by extension society more generally, views paedophilia. But in ancient Greece, as mentioned above, homosexual relations between men and boys didn't signal a 'deviant desire', a scandal or a crime, but an expression of friendship, a pedagogical practice (the ancients considered that knowledge was transferred from teachers to students in the sexual act), and a social (as much as an erotic) pleasure. An important basis for these different attitudes is that modern discourses of sexuality insist that it is in our sexual activity that the truth about our identity emerges, while the ancient Greeks saw it as just one of several social and aesthetic activities, and one that was not a big deal, not even as important or as interesting as food or exercise. Such variations in attitudes and understandings—and, of course, in social and political practice—means we have to acknowledge that sex is neither consistent nor, of itself, 'true'. Rather, it is just one way of engaging in social life, and its rules change with the changes in history and culture.

Sex and its context(s)

Discourses and attitudes also change within specific cultures over time. To go back to the ancient Greeks and their penchant for paedophilia, Foucault charts the way in which the 'love of boys' changed in that period. In early Greek writings it was an important practice, but later in antiquity new discourses ruled that abstinence was better than promiscuity, that sexual acts should be confined to the marital relationship, and that the point of sexual activity was not pleasure but procreation and the expression of affection between married partners. This came about not because the ancients suddenly decided that promiscuous sex was wrong, but as one aspect of a wider logic that focused on the importance of perfecting the self. To do this, so the discourses ran, sexual and other physical desires needed to be mastered and brought under the control of the rational nature. So the problem of sex was not how to prohibit it (as something sinful, harmful or disgusting), but how to manage it. And its focus was not, in the first instance, relations with others, but the relation with the self.

This signals a cross-over point between the care of the self and the care of others: the aim of abstinence, or restricted sex, was not to eliminate desire, but to balance one's physical desires with the needs of one's 'soul', and the reward was not just personal perfection, but the good of the whole community. The idea was that if everyone was rational and responsible, society would be based on reason rather than passion, and its members would respect one another and their mutual obligations. And what this was supposed to produce was a community marked by companionship, care and mutual kindness—a 'healthy' society. Mulder and Scully from television's *X-Files* are perhaps the best contemporary examples of ancient Greek sexual ethics. Although there is an obvious sexual tension between them (one of the selling points of the show, and its associated movie, has been whether they would 'do it') they never give in to their desire, and nor do they date other people. Rather, their libido is directed outwards—into finding the truth that is 'out there' so that the rest of us can be protected from aliens and from crazies—and their sexual abstinence allows them to focus on the production of a better, and a more ordered, society.

This attitude is very different from the bawdiness of medieval Europe, and of course from the Victorian age or our own, both of which are fascinated with sex and believe that sexuality is fundamental to the human condition. Over the centuries sex and discourses on sex have changed, and it has moved from being simply a physical and pleasurable act, to something associated with the perfecting of the self, to something sinful (associated with the emergence of the Christian era), and now to something that must be administered, a 'police' (or policy) matter. The idea that sex must be policed—subject to official policies—emerged in the eighteenth century, and from this point sex became public property. And, as public property, it became a potential resource that could be threatened or misused, and hence something that needed to be analysed by experts and managed by institutional authority rather than by people themselves.

Sexual subjects

To understand this shift from the ancient Greek approach to the present view, Foucault looks at the discursive changes more generally across these periods. Sex as we now understand it came out of the Enlightenment. And, as we saw in previous chapters, in this period the dominant attitude—the episteme—was a desire to classify and categorise, not to achieve self-mastery, but to achieve knowledge. This meant that sex was transformed from something physical into something discursive, something that must be understood scientifically. It also meant that sex was transferred from the sphere of 'family matters' to a place firmly within institutions because, as public property, it had to be studied, known and shaped in ways that were amenable to the interests of society.

One of the outcomes of this Enlightenment-based approach of classifying and naming particular sexualities was that new kinds of subjects were identified, and hence brought into existence. In pre-Enlightenment and pre-Victorian Europe, when people were punished for engaging in same-sex relations, committing adultery or having sex with animals, this was a punishment based on their sin or offence. They were not seen as being either sick or innately perverse—of having deviant subjectivities—but as people who had committed sins. But the assumption for the Victorians (and indeed under many contemporary jurisdictions) is that perverse or illegal acts make visible the subjectivity of the actor. The focus of institutional attention is not, in the first instance, the act—of homosexuality, of adultery or bestiality—but the state of being a homosexual, an adulterer or a pervert and, rather than punishing the act, it is the person who must be corrected and 'cured'. Rapists, for instance, are not sent to prison just to be punished or excluded from society—at least in those prisons that have a budget for therapy, the rapists have to attend counselling sessions, work out why they committed rape, and find better (healthier) ways of being.

So, from the Enlightenment, it became individuals and not just their acts that were classified as deviant, ethical, or normal, and the standards for this classification come out of contemporary discourses on sex. For much of the twentieth century, for instance, 'normal' people have been understood to be people who enter into heterosexual marriages, buy homes and raise children and household pets. Homosexuals and paedophiles have been marked as 'deviant', and punished, often brutally. Nuns and priests are seen as 'ethical' subjects because they choose to abstain from sex on religious grounds. Those who don't fit the pattern, especially other celibates (the bachelor uncle, for instance), are regarded with suspicion because they are not obviously deviant, or obviously ethical, and they are certainly not obviously 'normal'.

Power-knowledge

Using people's sexuality to classify their subjectivity is an important move, because it focuses attention on the person, rather than the act, and it establishes the grounds for people to be understood and explained as particular types of being, in a particular relation to themselves, their society and its norms. The various scandals associated with Bill Clinton's sex life are an example of this, because his public adulteries and his failure to confess and repent often enough or early enough have been used by members of the Republican party as evidence of his 'real' self. These representatives have argued that, regardless of his integrity in other fields and the successes he may have had as president, the fact that he lied about having an affair with a White House intern makes manifest the 'truth' of Bill Clinton—the truth that he is a liar, sexually ungoverned, and hence unworthy to administer the nation.

This association between truth and sexuality, and the production of the categories 'normal' and 'deviant', along with what Foucault sees as the almost obsessive interest that western societies have had in sex since the Victorian age, are based on what he calls 'power-knowledge'. These attitudes and regulatory practices emerged at the same time as the development of the social sciences, and they provided the emerging social sciences with objects of study. Demographics, economics and eugenics focused on 'normal' subjects—mainly married couples—because the interest here was in developing a database which could be used to measure levels of production and consumption against the birthrate. But, as is still the case, 'deviant' subjects received more attention from the experts (the scientists), partly because whatever is considered normal is also considered self-evident and not requiring of analysis, and partly because coding something as deviant, and forbidden, automatically makes it interesting.

Early psychoanalysts, for instance, were fascinated with what they termed 'hysterical women', and analysed them in terms of their failure to comply with the standards of the order of things—the position of women in society. Women who complained about being sexually molested by uncles, fathers and brothers, or who were dissatisfied with their secondary status, were typically classified as mad, deviant or sick, the victims of over-active imaginations or ungoverned desire. One popular treatment was to confine such women to bed, in a darkened room, to forbid them to read or do anything interesting, and to fatten them up until they were plump, calm and compliant. The legal and medical professions were also interested in the 'perverse adult', typically either homosexual men or promiscuous women, and in finding ways to treat them—for instance, by placing them in clinics or prisons. Medicine again, along with education, was concerned with children's masturbatory tendencies and finding strategies to control these. Young ladies were required to sleep with their hands above the blankets, for instance, and alternative outlets for boys' sexuality were found: the French novelist Proust writes that his father sent him off to a brothel in the hopes that 'normal' sex would cure his excessive masturbation.

Thus the body became the site, or the 'local centre', of power-knowledge under the surveillance of experts and authorised watchers, and the Victorian age—which we remember now as the period of the repression of sex—was actually the period when sex became highly visible. Rather than an absence of sex, we can see what Foucault calls an explosion of discourses on sex: it was 'not that they consigned sex to a shadow existence, but that they dedicated themselves to speaking about it *ad infinitum*, while exploiting it as *the* secret' (Foucault 1978: 35). And the focus of this discursive explosion was not to find better ways of engaging in sex, to drive sex out or to prohibit it, but rather to know it. So sex in the Modern age has been dominated by what Foucault calls a *scientia sexualis*, a focus on knowledge rather than pleasure, sex as a key to understanding subjects, and hence to achieving social wellbeing. He contrasts this with the other dominant way of understanding and dealing with sex, the *ars erotica*. This—exemplified by tantric sexual techniques—focuses on ways of intensifying pleasure, and works from the principle that truth is drawn from pleasure. *Scientia sexualis*, though, strips pleasure from the practice, and bases truth in scientific principles of classification, organisation and measurement.

We can see this dreary sexual attitude in a scene from the Monty Python movie *The Meaning of Life*, where John Cleese is teaching a class on sex education. The remorseless listing of erogenous zones and sexual techniques, along with the scolding of the boys when they fail to pay sufficient attention, denies any actual bodily pleasure in sex. Rather, sex is seen as a technology, and a site for regulation. When Cleese's 'wife' joins him to demonstrate sex to the schoolboys the scene becomes a sort of anti-pornography—a mechanical joyless activity, punctuated by explanations and everyday teacherly threats and warnings. This sort of sex is simply grim duty, performed according to strictly categorised norms, and in the interests of reproduction (of children, of knowledge). Contrast this with the erotic scene in *Dangerous Liaisons*, where the amoral main character initiates a young woman into sexual matters by constructing their activities as if they were school lessons ('Let's start with some Latin words . . .').

The rules of sex

An important effect of *scientia sexualis* is that systems of classifying and evaluating sexual practices are developed. We see this particularly in the way in which limits are placed on what is acceptable sexual practice. In Victoria's England, for instance, 'acceptable' sex was sex between heterosexual married couples, for the purpose of procreation. Other sexual practices were forbidden, denied or hidden. Foucault gives the example of children's sexuality to show how discourses change, and yet how powerful they can be in their own period. In the Middle Ages, for instance, people recognised that children were (or could be) sexually aware and even active, whether they considered this a good thing or not. But there was no place in Victorian discourses for children's sexuality, and so it was simultaneously forbidden and denied, even though this is patently illogical. 'Everyone knew', Foucault writes, 'that children had no sex, which was why they were forbidden to talk about it, why one closed one's eyes and stopped one's ears whenever they came to show evidence to the contrary' (1978: 4). And it was also why technologies—for instance, the invention of machines designed to prevent teenage boys from masturbating—were developed to ensure that children's sexuality (the sexuality that didn't exist) was regulated.

Although the rules were beginning to relax by the late 1990s, a similar attitude still exists. *Sesame Street* probably remains the preferred image of childhood in TV-land—innocence, cuteness, children learning in an environment of supportive and non-sexual adults. The cult show *South Park*, in dramatic contrast, shows children as sexual subjects, or at least as sexually aware people, people who understand what is involved in their Grade 2 teacher's fetishistic attachment to his glove puppet, or know how to negotiate adulterous parents and promiscuous city officials. But although this offers a very alternative view of children's sexuality, it is not a children's show as such: in Australia at least, it screens at the after-bedtime hour of 9:30 p.m. and is classified M—for mature audiences. In other words, the Victorian attitude that children don't have the sexuality they have still exists.

This sort of double-speak on sexuality had another interesting effect: the production of even more forms of perversity. The discursive and regulatory attention paid to sex and sexuality means that we are continually being called to focus on it, to think about what is approved and what is not. This makes sex very important—far more important than the ancient Greeks would have dreamed—and its association with right and wrong, with approved and forbidden, means that we are constantly tempted to test its limits. So the *scientia sexualis* and its evaluative classifications allowed the emergence of new ways of thinking about sex and doing sex, new ways of combining sexualities and thereby multiplying pleasures. This also brings into existence new subjectivities based on sexuality, new norms and standards, new discourses and new ways of being.

And here we can see another effect of discourses and institutional techniques that target sexuality: while they might seem coercive, Foucault would be at pains to emphasise that they are also productive. As we have seen, our subjectivities are to a considerable extent predicated on our sexuality. The discourses provide us with blueprints for how our (sexual) identities can be developed, and how we can navigate the social space successfully. Much of the content of adolescent girls' magazines, for instance, is directed to how sexual desires might properly be expressed and how readers can 'prove' themselves to be effective sexual beings. Movies which target adolescent boys similarly focus on their sexual subjectivity: films as different as *Small Faces* and *Encino Man* share the twin (apparently contradictory) themes of living hard and fast (chemical stimulants, aggressive music and casual sex) and developing socially and sexually responsible relationships. And, of course, this doesn't stop at adolescence: *Penthouse* mixes up explicit sexual photographs with reasoned articles about social and political practice, and women's magazines describe how to balance the sexy and the corporate 'look'.

So Foucault would not reject modern sexuality because it was coercive. Although in some ways and for some people it certainly is coercive, it also provides us with techniques for living. Where Foucault takes issue with modern sexuality is in its power to constrain us from acting, from explaining and exploring our selves in alternative fashions. But in the decades since Foucault began his major work on sexuality, those discourses and techniques that can be traced back to Victorian principles have begun to be changed by contemporary practice. Although, as Foucault's earlier work points out, power is able to constrain us, his later work shows that we are able to resist, reject or deflect power. While power may be everywhere, it can't control everything, and it can't operate according to a single logic.

As we have seen, direct prohibition doesn't effectively control behaviour, because the more the network of rules and regulatory devices increases, the less possible it is to successfully police all of its aspects; and the more that people explore prohibited or controlled practices, the more those practices become 'normal'. For instance, until fairly recently it was considered wrong—sinful, irresponsible, inappropriate—for a couple to live in a marital relationship without possessing a formal marriage licence. Such couples were 'living in sin' and they and their children were denied both respectability and a range of social and economic benefits. But increasingly over the past few decades, as more couples reject the legal or formal aspect of marriage, de facto relationships have come to be treated as legally accepted, at least for the purposes of income tax and social security assessments. Even the British royal family has been touched by this, so that Prince Charles' adultery with Camilla Parker-Bowles—which in an earlier generation would have been silenced or forbidden—has begun to be framed in the media and the public eye as a long-term commitment, 'true love', an authorised relationship. In other words, although social and institutional discourses and their related technologies formulate our subjectivity, they are themselves social effects, and respond to changes in social practices. What is right or ethical in any given period is simply what fits the dominant episteme, and is authorised by the discourses and institutions in which the practice is framed.

Sex and ethics

This brings us to the final issue we will explore with regard to sex and sexuality, and that is the question of ethics. In Foucault's definition, 'morality' refers to sets of rules and prohibitions—the codes of a society—while 'ethics' refers to the values these rules ascribe to different behaviours, and to how people behave in relation to these rules. And an important aspect of both moral or ethical behaviour is that it is a technology for regulating social relations and the relationship with the self.

In the present period, with the death of God and of the author (and when the nation-state and the global economy aren't looking too healthy either) there is no generally shared basis for moral or ethical precepts. One of the reasons Foucault finds sexuality a fertile site in which to examine ethics is because of its connection to subjectivity, which means that it is one of the few remaining sites for ethical behaviour. But, as we have seen, there are multiple, changing, and often contradictory rules associated with sex and sexuality, and this means it is not always easy to identify when a rule has been broken. The connections between moral, legal and ethical positions on sex and sexuality are very unstable, and Foucault certainly doesn't attempt to produce a general ethics, but points out that ethical systems are determined by their social contexts, by the sorts of knowledge that are valid in a particular context, and by relations of power.

Again, the issue of children's sexuality is a useful way of exploring ethics. We described earlier the weighty mechanisms used to catch and punish paedophiles; the discourses employed in police and media reports circulated around the idea of 'protection'. But it is not clear, in the paedophilia case, whether it was living breathing children, or the idea of childhood (as a state of sexless innocence), that was being protected: surely actual children are more endangered by, say, the need to work in the sex industry because of their poverty than by paedophiles looking at pornographic photographs. And, certainly, the idea of childhood is easier to deal with in ethical and judicial terms than are actual children, because the legal grounds for establishing who is a child, what constitutes a breach of their innocence, and on what criteria this should be regulated, are murky. For instance, in 1989 a Canadian judge ruled that a man who molested his toddler stepdaughter should be considered less culpable because the child was sexually precocious. He subsequently came under severe public criticism, since current legal and moral standards hold that a pre-pubescent (and virtually pre-linguistic) child shouldn't be sexually active, certainly not with an adult, and most certainly not with a stepfather, in fact, it is the moral responsibility of the adult to curb any such actions of the child. For older stepchildren, though, these rules may be relaxed. Woody Allen, for example, did nothing illegal by marrying his stepdaughter, though it was considered morally suspect in many circles. However, an eighteen-year-old who has sex with a post-pubescent fifteen-year-old may be legally criminal, but not everyone would consider that an immoral act had been committed.

Conclusion

This convoluted material, and its moral and legal uncertainty, is critical to Foucault's work on sexuality and subjectivity because he argues that it is in the relation with the self, rather than in what one does to others, that the individual practices ethics. As we have seen in this chapter, Foucault's writings on the sexual subject show that:

- sex and sexuality are as much to do with discourses and ideas as with bodily activities or erotic desires;
- what constitutes sex, how it should happen, where and with whom is determined by its social and historical contexts;
- sex is both the site for the practice of what Foucault calls 'power-knowledge', and for the exercise of ethics by the individuals concerned;
- ethical practice, for Foucault, is not that which complies with a moral or legal code, but is 'the practice of freedom'—the act of making a deliberate choice to construct oneself as an ethical subject, in relation to the self and to others.

This sounds very close to the ancient Greek approach to sexuality and ethics, but it is one which is far more accommodating of sexual and social differences. And, where the ancient Greeks were driven by the desire to achieve perfection, Foucault's concern is to find ways of understanding ourselves as moral subjects with moral obligations who can develop and deploy technologies of the self—'arts of the self'—by which we can constitute ourselves as subjects, and live beautiful lives. In the next chapter we deal with Foucault's work on ethics as a series of techniques, practices and policies by which the self—and by extension, the society—can be constructed as a work of art.

Further reading

Butler, Judith 1990, *Gender Trouble: Feminism and the Subversion of Identity*, Routledge, London, see Chapter 3

McNay, Lois 1992, *Foucault and Feminism: Power, Gender and the Self*, North-eastern University Press, Boston, see Chapter 2

Foucault, Michel 1985, *The History of Sexuality: Vol. 2, The Use of Pleasure*, Penguin, Harmondsworth

10

Arts of the self

> What strikes me is the fact that, in our society, art has
> become something related only to objects and not to
> individuals or to life. That art is something which is
> specialized or done by experts who are artists. But
> couldn't everyone's life become a work of art? Why
> should the lamp or the house be an art object but not
> our life? (Foucault 1997: 261)

This chapter concludes our discussion of Foucault's notions
of the subject by looking at his later writings, where he shifts
his focus from the effects of power to the ways in which
human beings become 'subjects'. An important concept that
comes out of this work is that the self can be 'authored' by
us, the subjects, and that we can produce these selves and our
lives as works of art. Foucault's early work on subjectivity
effectively debunked the idea that identity is inherent or
natural, but it failed to explain how and why individuals can
in fact act autonomously, or resist the power of disciplinary
forces and institutional discourses. In his later work he argues
that individuals can in fact 'cultivate' themselves through
what he calls 'arts of existence' that not only allow us to
become self-determining agents, but also provide the grounds
for us to challenge and resist power structures.

While this represents a substantial departure from his
earlier writings (that the self is a docile body, produced by

dominant discourses and institutions), he does not set the subject free to be just anything. Rather, he outlines the ways in which privileged and privileging discourses of the subject and of aesthetics (taste and style) help determine what sorts of self can be authored. So, while these later writings on the subject go a considerable distance to retrieving the concept of ethics and self-reflexivity, they do not establish a free-for-all in which anything goes. Power-knowledge, contexts and discourses still limit the possibilities of subjectivity—both of who we can be and the kinds of relations that are possible with ourselves and with others.

We will outline his work on this self-reflexive, ethical subject by discussing technologies of authoring (the self, a book, an arts policy) and the conditions under which individual subjects become authors in these various senses. We will also look at the field of art, and particularly the ways in which its discourses establish and normalise our understandings of truth and beauty, and hence how and what we 'choose' to author.

Authorship and subjectivity

The subject, Foucault writes, 'is not a substance. It is a form' (1997: 290). And as a form, it both can be, and must be, crafted, a crafting that occurs within specific social contexts, and with regard to particular mores and truths. Foucault's perspective here comes out of his archaeology of subjectivity and ethics, from antiquity to the present. As we have discussed in previous chapters, in this work he uncovered a series of moral systems, a variety of ways of understanding how the self should relate to itself and to others, and a range of bases for these ethics (God, social good, self-respect). The fact that there is no consistency and no universality in either our understandings or our practices over these millennia, he argues, raises two important points. First, as we have already seen, the subject is social and historical rather than innate. And, second, the differences in what constitutes a subject—and the possibility of change, despite social and historical limits—demonstrates the exercise of freedom. 'Modern man . . .' Foucault writes, 'is the man who tries to invent himself. This modernity does not "liberate man in his own being"; it compels him to face the task of producing himself' (Foucault 1984b: 42). So we aren't just inherently what we are, and we aren't just made what we are by powerful discourses and institutions; as Madonna has shown us over the past decade or so, we can be (within limits) what we decide to be, and we can change that being when it no longer suits.

Foucault turns to the world of artistic production to develop an understanding of this new idea of the subject because, as he argues, it is 'the author'—by which we mean any creative agent, whether writer, painter, filmmaker or theorist—that allows us to conceive of the subject as a specific and particular individual, someone who can be distinguished from all other subjects. This is very different from conventional 'scientific' forms of classification because, unlike the difference between, say, one rock and another (size, shape, weight, colour, consistency), we can identify particular authors by their particular and peculiar ways of communicating their own sets of values, ideas and ways of seeing the world. We understand, for instance, that Platonic thought is very different from Marxist theory, and presume from this that Plato was an entirely different person from Marx. Even if we have had no training in art, we can tell the difference between a work by Picasso and, say, Botticelli, and understand from that difference something about the character, the values and the world-view of each artist. Closer to home, although most of us will never meet either Quentin Tarantino or Steven Spielberg, we can identify them as particular individuals on the basis of their films, and on this basis we attribute to them particular personalities, and particular qualities of identity. And these authors manage, in a way, to escape time and acquire a kind of permanence because writing (or painting, or sculpture, or scientific discovery) separates the author from time. Think of Shakespeare, for instance. He has been dead for several hundred years but because his works still exist, and because he is inscribed in those works—in a sense is still alive—he has been able to outlive 'real' time. And whenever we accept the notion that an author is active and present in a body of writing (or film, or painting, or whatever), we also accept the notion that that author is a discrete and consistent subject, who can be distinguished from all other subjects.

This is a basis for the still widely-held notion that we each possess an authentic and individual self. But it is this authentic self that has come under fire from theorists (including Foucault) over much of the twentieth century. Roland Barthes, for instance, famously proclaimed 'the death of the author' in the middle of the twentieth century, and schools of literary and artistic criticism since then have trained students to ignore the history and character of the author or artist when analysing a text, and instead focus on the text as a 'thing itself', as something self-contained and divorced from the person who produced it. So, whereas previously students were encouraged to analyse a text by thinking about who wrote (or painted) it, and about the degree of originality and authenticity that can be found in the text, now students are exhorted to pay attention to the mode of existence of a text— What sort of a thing is it? What was its status when it was made? How does it relate to other social or cultural objects?— and to the discourses in which the text was produced. The 'unique subject' of the author is swallowed up by the social and discursive formations, and the important question becomes not 'who', but 'how'. 'And behind all these questions', Foucault writes, 'we would hear hardly anything but the stirring of an indifference: What difference does it make who is speaking?' (1998: 222).

The author function

Outside the academy, though, it does make a difference, and the author is still very much alive. It is the name of the author that sells books or that attracts us to movies—John Grisham's name is typically far more prominent on the covers of his paperback novels than the titles, and a movie is promoted as 'the new film by George Lucas'. It is also the author's name that authenticates knowledge and founds new disciplines: *Newtonian* physics, *Freudian* analysis, *Marxist* history and *Foucaultian* theory. Foucault calls this 'the author function', the necessary thing that marks a particular discourse or set of discourses and authorises them to circulate within a society. 'Author' in this sense doesn't in the first instance refer to the concrete person, but to the 'name' by which we know that particular writings and discourses are capital-'W' Works—literary writings, science, policy. How can we tell the difference between a shopping list and a poem, for instance, or a film and a home video? In some cases, only by the fact that the author's name is appended to the capital-'W' Work. This, Foucault suggests, is one reason why the author simply refuses to die.

Foucault uses this notion of author function to chart the changing status of the subject, because the way in which we currently understand the author function has not always been the case. In fact, it isn't universal even today. The writers of the average government report, for instance, however literary their ambitions, and however much they may labour over their prose and syntax, disappear when it is published. Even though none of us actually believe that a being called the Ministry of Finance sat down and wrote a report, the Ministry is still the only authorised author and owner of the text. Individual subjects aren't important to bureaucracies. Similarly, the subject as we now understand it didn't exist in the Middle Ages, as we can see in everyday practices such as storytelling. No authors existed (or rather, were recognised and recorded) for fictional texts in this period; instead, the stories circulated as collectively owned pieces of writing— hence the enormous number of ballads written by the mysterious 'Anon.'. Still, the subject was beginning to emerge in the Middle Ages, as we can see in the fact that, unlike literary works, scientific texts produced in this period needed the author function. They were only considered 'true' if they could be clearly identified with an originator, the author-subject, someone who was able to penetrate the order of things, and clarify and classify the 'raw stuff' of nature. This had changed by the Classical age; now scientific texts were only classed as valid if their truths could be demonstrated, and not because of their association with the scientist-author. Interestingly, at the same time the reverse happened with literary texts: now texts by Anon. were no longer considered valuable or valid, and the truth of literary works was tied back to the name of the author.

In any event, in each period the author lurked—and still lurks—in the text: either by being effaced under the guise of 'scientific truth' or 'collective ownership', or by being the visible principle of legitimation of the text. This makes it difficult to insist that the author is dead, or that fictions can be read as purely internal structures: any text is always mediated by the presence of the author's name, and the status and function of that name in the society. But of course how the author-subject functions in history is determined by the social context, including the technologies and infrastructure available.

Technologies of the subject-author

One important precondition for the modern subject, Foucault argues, is alphabetical writing. There are really only two ways of rendering speech in writing; one is the abstract alphabet we now use, and the other is a system of ideograms or pictograms. The latter is what was used for most of history (and indeed still is, in some parts of the world). Unlike alphabetical writing, pictograms point directly to the things they represent—for instance, the idea of 'person' might be rendered by a stick drawing of a person, and the word 'song' by a drawing of a bird alongside a mouth. We could say that pictograms are once removed from the thing they signify.

Alphabetical writing is very different in its approach to signification. The letters and words that make up a written sentence don't in any way resemble what they represent, but are twice removed from the thing signified. What this means is that the alphabet takes us one step away from the concrete world of objects, and constructs a world of abstract squiggles—a world of representation, rather than the 'real'. And while the 'real' is still there (no matter how we render the word 'stone' in writing, and no matter what we say about its status, a stone dropped on my head is still going to hurt), this distance that emerges between the concrete world and the world of representation allows us to understand that things are not always the same, not always identical to themselves, but can be represented in a variety of ways.

So, Foucault argues, alphabetical writing provides the grounds for current understandings of the subject—not something real, permanent or unchangeable, but the variable, and somewhat fictional, subject of representation. Diana, the late Princess of Wales, is a case in point. If we relied on pictograms for stories about Diana, we would have only a series of sketches of blonde hair, tilted head and kohl-lined eyes. But, as the media has so comprehensively reported over the past decade or so, we have a myriad representations of subject-Diana: fairy-tale princess, neurotic screamer, loving mother, betrayed lover, wily manipulator, courageous reformer and, finally, broken saint. And we can identify Diana in each story, but also recognise the enormous number of facets and narratives associated with subject-Diana. She is at once herself, distinguished from a thousand other blonde tilted-headed women, and all kinds of selves, something that couldn't be achieved (or with far greater difficulty) in a system of pictograms.

The world of the artist-subject

So artistic or creative production, and the infrastructure and conditions that support it, have been complicit with the development of the modern subject. But, as we saw earlier in our discussion of the author function, this position of author/ artist, and contexts available to them, have not been consistent across history. The development of the idea that artists are individual, special and privileged (the creative genius) has been gradual. In pre-literate Christian Europe, the mode of communication was what Foucault calls direct resemblance— what would be pictograms, for written communication—and a direct relationship was assumed to exist between the telling of something and what it represents (what you see is what you get). Artists were, for the most part, simply anonymous people who sketched or performed or narrated the lives and triumphs of epic heroes. It was the story, not the storyteller, that was important. Rather than unique or particular identities presenting a personal view of the world, they were considered artisans, anonymous people working with a set of skills.

The changing world of the Renaissance, including the breaking up of the old guilds and the rise of universities and scientific reason, meant a change in the status of artists. He (usually, but not inevitably, he) was understood as hero—as more important than the story—because his works gave ordinary people access to new worlds and new ways of seeing. Artists began to separate themselves from the everyday workforce, galleries began to be established, systems of patronage developed, and the special genius-artist we now know began to come into being.

These social, discursive and institutional changes were preconditions for the emergence not just of the artist, but of the modern subject more generally. But it wasn't until the eighteenth century that art and literature took on the character they have now: as objects produced not, in the first instance, to make money or to communicate directly, but to explore sensibilities, and to express and reflect abstract concepts. And again, this was tied to the mode of representation. Instead of demanding that 'good' artistic works directly resemble the thing represented, the new idea was that the works represented some truth about the thing represented, as a way of affirming the value and order of the universe. Certainly artists were understood as discrete subjects, but the dominant discourses were still of truth and essential qualities.

By the nineteenth century, though, artists had begun to reject representation of things and, instead, began to focus on 'the things of representation'—styles and techniques, ways of seeing and being. Impressionist paintings, for instance, were not so much concerned with the thing represented as with the form of representation—how light was rendered, how to explore feelings in paint—and this sort of approach allowed artists to move away from the notion that there is just one right way of seeing and being. Contemporary works have moved even further from resemblance, and from ways of alluding to the 'real' world. One example is the abstraction of American minimalism in the middle of the twentieth century, when a work might be only a streak of paint on a white canvas, and where art refused to represent the world at all. From a different approach, but with a similar attitude, we can think of the extreme self-reflexivity of contemporary art, where works refer only to the art world—to other works of art, to traditions, to politics and practice in galleries. In either case what we have is, like René Magritte's famous *This is not a pipe*, artists refusing to affirm anything—truth, beauty, concrete reality—or to make any final truth claims.

Art in society

These shifts in understandings of creative production and of the subject have not happened automatically or in a vacuum. Whether we choose to examine painting, or literature, or scientific writing, or government policies, the ways in which things are said, their connection to concrete experience, and their reception in the public sphere are determined by the social context and the infrastructure in which they are made and circulated. For instance, it wouldn't have been possible for writing to take on the privileged position it now has without most of the population being literate. And the moves from resemblance to representation to abstraction couldn't have happened unless people generally were able to think in those ways. Style, subject matter and the form of any creative production are always part of a wider set of discursive and institutional technologies. Where they have been utterly at odds with the dominant discourses, they have either been ignored or repressed. Vincent van Gogh, for example, was virtually ignored in his own lifetime, though he is now one of the more significant artists in the western canon. For more recent examples we can think of work by artists like Robert Mapplethorpe and Andres Serrano: in the United States and on tour elsewhere they have generated enormous interest, debate, outrage, government intervention, and even physical violence. This is because, while their form—representational photography—is perfectly acceptable, what they have chosen to represent, and how they present it, is not. Mapplethorpe's homo-erotic or sado-masochistic photographs, for instance, may have been perfectly acceptable in a psychology textbook, to illustrate a discussion of perverse sexuality. But because they are aestheticised, and presented as art, they become regarded as a form of perversion themselves. And Serrano's most famous and most controversial photograph, *Piss Christ*, is a very beautiful picture of a crucifix, one that without its title could well hang on the wall of any convent. But because he combines 'piss' and 'Christ', and because we know that he photographed the crucifix in a vial of his own urine, many people consider it objectionable, offensive, sacrilegious. In some venues the funding or management bodies have banned exhibitions of these works altogether. And in others, huge crowds—including protest groups—have attended, attracted by the scandal. But, in either event, the exhibitions are not easily allowed to proceed as art—being either banned or with access to the shows being restricted. At the National Gallery in Melbourne, Australia, the 1997 exhibition of Serrano's work closed early in the interests of public and staff safety.

Aesthetics and ethics

Foucault insists that there is a connection between aesthetics and subjectivity. He writes, 'the transformation of one's self by one's own knowledge is, I think, something rather close to the aesthetic experience. Why should a painter work if he is not transformed by his own painting?' (1997: 131). And, as Foucault's many analyses of art and literature point out, aesthetics is not only for the elite, but is a part of social practice more generally. Not only is it one of the sites in which the modern subject has been able to emerge; it is also one of the ways of organising and regulating populations, and of determining what can be said and how it can be said. In other words, the world of art and aesthetics has an influence in determining what is understood to be true. And, as we saw in relation to Mapplethorpe and Serrano, a great deal of energy, and often of hostility or outright conflict, goes into establishing just what a picture should represent, what topics a novel should deal with, how much sex and violence is appropriate in a film and, in short, what are the appropriate forms for representations of 'the truth'. Aesthetics, far from being a decadent bourgeois pursuit, is something in which everyone participates, and in which we all have a stake. The fact that people can say 'I don't know much about art, but I know what I like' indicates the extent to which subjects, trained or untrained, bourgeois or working class, claim a right to judge works of art—and not just the works, but the forms of representation used to produce them. As Foucault writes, 'people cling to ways of seeing, saying, doing, and thinking, more than to what is seen, to what is thought, said, or done' (1998: 242). We see this in the surprising levels of hostility directed to new movements in the art world, with grunge novels, for instance, rejected as 'disgusting' or 'encouraging suicide', and non-representational paintings called 'not art'.

An effect of the importance of aesthetics to society is that, across what is usually referred to as the western world, governments write art and cultural policies, fund art and artists, and generally regulate the field, attempting to ensure that the right sort of works are made, by the right sort of people, for the right audiences. One reason governments pay attention to art, of course, is economic, since the field of arts provides employment for a surprisingly large number of people, and produces a respectable percentage of the gross national product. But, perhaps more importantly, art is associated with ethics, with meaning, with ways of representing ourselves to ourselves and to others, and with the telling of 'truths' about society and its members. Because of this, arts policy is both a technology for managing and normalising populations (by producing authorised ways of representing 'us'), and a way of producing ethical subjects (by ensuring that we develop 'good' taste).

The association between aesthetics and ethics is not new. For the Stoics in ancient Greece, for example, aesthetics was considered an ethics, and people (actually, only the elite) followed 'arts of existence' not because they were imposed as rules, but because people chose to live ethically in order to create for themselves a beautiful life. Foucault picks up on this concept where he describes 'arts of the self' as:

> . . . those intentional and voluntary actions by which men
> not only set themselves rules of conduct, but also seek
> to transform themselves, to change themselves in their
> singular being, and to make their life into an oeuvre that
> carries certain aesthetic values and meets certain stylistic
> criteria. (1985: 10–11)

At this point, Foucault loses a lot of his supporters. His development of the idea of the self as a work of art, some critics assert, is based on a judgement of taste and privileges beauty over intellectual or moral virtues. It also, they assert, depoliticises people by encouraging a focus on the private self, rather than on engaging in wider social and political activities. And they argue that the 'arts of the self' can only be enjoyed by those who have the time and money to focus self-indulgently on themselves.

Certainly there is a degree of self-interest in our attempts to apply an aesthetics of existence: we write to be loved, Foucault says. But, as he writes elsewhere, art and judgements of taste aren't divorced from the wider community, and the arts, or practices of the self are 'not something that the individual invents by himself. They are patterns that he finds in his culture and which are proposed, suggested and imposed on him by his culture, his society and his social group' (1984b: 11). From this standpoint, we can suggest, individuals who are involved in the arts of the self, in producing themselves as subjects and their lives as works of art, are neither self-indulgent nor free agents. While they may be applying an ethical perspective to ensure that they live as well as possible and, in the process, are able to benefit others, they are also products of their society and its polity.

We can see this most easily in the lives of celebrities who, perhaps more than most of us—and certainly more publicly than most of us—have lives that are works of art, and while they may attempt to make social and political changes, they are also products of their culture. Diana, Princess of Wales, again provides a well-known example of this effect—indeed, everything we know about her suggests that she had read her Foucault. Before the famous photograph of Diana Spencer cuddling a couple of toddlers while the sun shone through her skirt, she was any anonymously attractive young woman. But the photograph, announcing her imminent insertion into the British royal family, also marked her emergence as a celebrity—as someone who was both a product of the media and of social and institutional discourses, and an active agent in the production of her own identity—someone whose life was to be a work of art.

Clearly, Diana was able to use the media and her institutional connections to craft herself as a particular kind of subject—an ethical subject, an aesthetic subject, a political subject. Her hair, wardrobe, changing waistline, romances and very public visits to hospitals and war zones, as well as exercise gyms and night-clubs, all contributed to a life that was very much a work of art. But, equally clearly, she was a product, and continues to be well after her death: her image still guarantees the sale of magazines, newspapers and china dolls. Her ability to author herself—to craft her life as a work of art and to exercise an influence on the society and polity of Britain (affecting the status of the royal family, restrictions on press freedoms, support for the banning of landmines)—

depended on the social system in which she emerged. Without the press, without public fascination with celebrities, and without good beauty advisors she would have been just another important man's wife—perhaps still working on the construction of an ethical and a beautiful life, but very much on a personal and private level.

Conclusion

What we can take out of this example is Foucault's point that what lies behind the effort involved in taking care of the self, applying techniques of the self, and crafting one's life as a work of art is the relation between freedom and power. Aesthetics is important not because it is a bourgeois practice, or because beauty is inherently important. Rather, Foucault writes, the idea of aesthetics can be used as a metaphor for the self, and can provide a set of practices in and by which to take care of the self. By engaging so actively with our lives, we can exercise power in our own networks, making a world where, though I may not be a celebrity, I can still be the star of my own movie. This is, of course, an art of self-preoccupation, which 'emphasizes the importance of developing all the practices and all the exercises by which one can maintain self-control and eventually arrive at a pure enjoyment of oneself' (Foucault 1986a: 238). But in the intensification of the relationship of the self to itself—whether it be in sex, in pleasure, in aesthetics or in family relations—Foucault argues, and in presenting our lives as works of art, we can become better able to take responsibility for others, and to ensure harmony in our engagement with the broader community.

We have examined Foucault's writing on art and aesthetics through discussing:

- the changing status of 'the author' and the author-function, and what this means in terms of power-knowledge;

- the dependence of modes of representation on broader social conditions—levels of literacy, generalised beliefs, discursive norms;
- the importance of art and aesthetics in allowing the development of an ethics of the self.

Further reading

Bourdieu, Pierre 1993, *The Field of Cultural Production*, Polity Press, Cambridge (UK), see Chapter 1

Foucault, Michel 1984a, *The Final Foucault*, eds James Bernauer and David Rasmussen, MIT Press, Cambridge, Mass, see 'The ethic of the care for the self'

Staniszewski, Mary Anne 1995, *Believing is Seeing: Creating the Culture of Art*, Penguin, Harmondsworth

Bibliography

Publications by Foucault

——1961, *Folie et déraison: histoire de la folie à l'âge classique*, English edn 1982 *Madness and Civilization: a History of Insanity in the Age of Reason*, trans. Richard Howard, Tavistock, London

——1963, *Naissance de la clinique: une archéologie du regard médical*, English edn 1975 *The Birth of the Clinic: An Archaeology of Medical Perception*, trans. A.M. Sheridan Smith, Vintage, New York

——1966, *Les mots et les choses: une archéologie des sciences humaines*, English edn 1973 *The Order of Things: An Archaeology of the Human Sciences*, Vintage, New York

——1969, *L'Archéologie du savoir*, English edn 1972 *The Archaeology of Knowledge*, trans. A.M. Sheridan Smith, Pantheon Books, New York

——1975, *Surveiller et punir: naissance de la prison*, English edn 1995 *Discipline and Punish: the Birth of the Prison*, trans. Alan Sheridan, Vintage, New York

——1976, *Histoire de la sexualité, Vol. 1, La Volonté de savoir*, English edn 1978 *The History of Sexuality: Vol. 1, an Introduction*, trans. Robert Hurley, Penguin, Harmondsworth

——1980, *Power/Knowledge: Selected Interviews and Other Writings*, ed. Colin Gordon, Pantheon Books, New York

——1984, *Histoire de la sexualité, Vol. 2, L'Usage des plaisirs*, English edn 1985 *The History of Sexuality: Vol. 2, The Use of Pleasure*, trans. Robert Hurley, Penguin, Harmondsworth

——1984, *Histoire de la sexualité, Vol. 3, Le Souci de soi*, English edn 1986 *The History of Sexuality: Vol. 3, The Care of the Self*, trans. Robert Hurley, Penguin, Harmondsworth

——1984a, *The Final Foucault*, eds James Bernauer and David Rasmussen, MIT Press, Cambridge, Mass.

——1984b, *The Foucault Reader*, ed. Paul Rabinow, Penguin, London

——1986, *Language, Counter-Memory, Practice*, ed. Donald Bouchard, Cornell University Press, Ithaca

——1988, *Michel Foucault: Politics, Philosophy, Culture*, ed. Lawrence Kreitzman, Routledge, New York

——1991, *Remarks on Marx*, trans. James Goldstein and James Cascaito, Semiotext(e), New York

——1997, *Ethics: Essential Works of Foucault 1954–1984, Vol. 1*, ed. Paul Rabinow, Penguin, London

——1998, *Aesthetics, Method, and Epistemology: Essential Works of Foucault 1954–1984, Vol. 2*, ed. James Faubion, New Press, New York

General publications

Althusser, Louis 1977, *Lenin and Philosophy and Other Essays*, trans. Ben Brewster, New Left Books, London

Bachelard, Gaston 1984, *The New Scientific Spirit*, trans. Arthur Goldhammer, Beacon Press, Boston

Barthes, Roland 1979, *Image-Music-Text*, trans. Stephen Heath, Fontana/Collins, Glasgow

Baudrillard, Jean 1987, *Forget Foucault*, Semiotext(e), New York

Bersani, Leo 1986, *The Freudian Body*, Columbia University Press, New York

Best, Steven and Kellner, Douglas 1991, *Postmodern Theory: Critical Interrogations*, Macmillan, London

Bhabha, Homi 1994, *The Location of Culture*, Routledge, London

Bourdieu, Pierre 1989, *Distinction*, trans. Richard Nice, Routledge, London

——1990, *The Logic of Practice*, trans. Richard Nice, Polity Press, Cambridge, UK

——1991, *Language and Symbolic Power*, trans. Gino Raymond and Mathew Adamson, Polity Press, Cambridge, UK

——1993, *The Field of Cultural Production*, Polity Press, Cambridge, UK

——1998, *Practical Reason*, Polity Press, Cambridge, UK

Bourdieu, Pierre et al. 1994, *Academic Discourse*, trans. Richard Teese, Polity Press, Cambridge, UK

Burchell, Graham et al. (eds) 1991, *The Foucault Effect: Studies in Governmentality*, University of Chicago Press, Chicago

Butler, Judith 1987, *Subjects of Desire*, Columbia University Press, New York

——1990, *Gender Trouble: Feminism and the Subversion of Identity*, Routledge, London

——1993, *Bodies that Matter*, Routledge, New York

——1997a, *Excitable Speech*, Routledge, New York

Bibliography

———1997b, *The Psychic Life of Power*, Stanford University Press, Stanford

Canguilhem, Georges 1978, *The Normal and the Pathological*, trans. Carolyn Fawcett, Zone Books, New York

———1988, *Ideology and Rationality in the History of the Life Sciences*, trans. Arthur Goldhammer, MIT Press, Cambridge, Mass.

Certeau, Michel de 1984, *The Practice of Everyday Life*, trans. Steven Rendall, University of California Press, Berkeley

———1986, *Heterologies: Discourse on the Other*, trans. Brian Massumi, University of Minnesota Press, Minneapolis

———1988, *The Writing of History*, trans. Tom Conley, Columbia University Press, New York

Clark, C.M.H, 1962, *A History of Australia, Vol. 1: From the Earliest Times to the Age of Macquarie*, Melbourne University Press, Melbourne

Deleuze, Gilles 1988, *Foucault*, trans. Sean Hand, Athlone Press, London

Dreyfus, Hubert and Rabinow, Paul 1986, *Michel Foucault: Beyond Structuralism and Hermeneutics*, Harvester Press, Brighton, UK

Eribon, Didier 1991, *Michel Foucault*, Faber, London

Freud, Sigmund 1987, *On Metapsychology: The Theory of Psychoanalysis*, ed. Angela Richards, trans. James Strachey, Penguin, Harmondsworth

Frow, John 1995, *Cultural Studies and Cultural Value*, Clarendon Press, Oxford

Gramsci, Antonio 1986, *Selections from Prison Notebooks*, eds and trans. Quinton Hoare and Geoffrey Smith, Lawrence and Wishart, London

Gregory, Derek 1994, *Geographical Imaginations*, Blackwell, Oxford

Grosz, Elizabeth 1994, *Volatile Bodies*, Allen & Unwin, Sydney

Hegel, Georg 1956, *The Philosophy of History*, trans. J Sibree, Dover, New York

———1967, *The Phenomenology of Spirit*, trans. A. Miller, Clarendon Press, Oxford

Heidegger, Martin 1990, *Being and Time*, trans. John Macquarrie and Edward Robinson, Blackwell, Oxford

Hughes, Robert 1993, *Culture of Complaint: The Fraying of America*, Oxford University Press, New York

Kojeve, Alexandre 1986, *Introduction to the Reading of Hegel*, ed. Allan Bloom, trans. James Nichols, Cornell University Press, Ithaca

Kuhn, Thomas 1970, *The Structure of Scientific Revolutions*, University of Chicago Press, Chicago

Lacan, Jacques 1977, *Ecrits: A Selection*, trans. Alan Sheridan, Norton, New York

Lodge, David 1988, *Nice Work*, Penguin, London

Marx, Karl 1967, *Writings of the Young Marx on Philosophy and Society*, eds and trans. Loyd Easton and Kurt Guddat, Doubleday, New York

———1981, *Surveys from Exile*, ed. David Fernbach, Penguin, Harmondsworth

———1995, *Capital*, ed. David McLellan, Oxford University Press, Oxford

Marx, Karl and Engels, Friedrich 1988, *The Communist Manifesto*, Penguin, Harmondsworth

McNay, Lois 1992, *Foucault and Feminism: Power, Gender and the Self*, Northeastern University Press, Boston

——1994, *Foucault: A Critical Introduction*, Continuum, New York

Merleau-Ponty, Maurice 1992, *Phenomenology of Perception*, trans. Colin Smith, Routledge, London

Nietzsche, Friedrich 1956, *The Birth of Tragedy and The Genealogy of Morals*, trans. Francis Golffing, Doubleday, New York

——1968, *The Will to Power*, ed. Walter Kaufman, trans. Walter Kaufman and R.J. Hollingdale, Vintage, New York

——1974, *The Gay Science*, trans. Walter Kaufman, Vintage Books, New York

O'Farrell, Clare (ed.) 1997, *Foucault: The Legacy*, QUT Press, Brisbane

Pateman, Carole 1988, *The Sexual Contract*, Polity Press, Cambridge, UK

Patton, Paul (ed.) 1993, *Nietzsche, Feminism and Political Theory*, Allen & Unwin, Sydney

Ransom, John 1997, *Foucault's Discipline: The Politics of Subjectivity*, Duke University Press, Durham and London

Said, Edward 1978, *Orientalism*, Penguin, London

Schirato, Tony and Yell, Susan 1996, *Communication and Cultural Literacy: An Introduction*, Allen & Unwin, Sydney

Staniszewski, Mary Anne 1995, *Believing is Seeing: Creating the Culture of Art*, Penguin, Harmondsworth

Stoler, Ann 1995, *Race and the Education of Desire*, Duke University Press, Durham

Virilio, Paul 1991, *The Lost Dimension*, trans. Daniel Moshenberg, Semiotext(e), New York

Young, Robert 1990, *White Mythologies: Writing History and the West*, Routledge, London

Index